Friends Way 1

George Fox's journey

Martin Budgett
Jacquetta Megarry

Rucksack Readers

Friends Way 1: George Fox's journey

First published 2022

Rucksack Readers, 6 Old Church Lane, Edinburgh EH15 3PX, UK

Phone   +44/0131 661 0262

Email: *info@rucsacs.com*

Website   *www.rucsacs.com*

ISBN: 978-1-913817-06-0

British Library cataloguing in publication data: a catalogue record for this book is available from the British Library.

Designed in Scotland by Ian Clydesdale (ian@clydesdale.scot)

Printed and bound in the UK by Short Run Press, Exeter on rainproof, biodegradable paper.

FSC
www.fsc.org
MIX
Paper from
responsible sources
FSC® C014540

Publisher's note

You are responsible for your own safety when using the Way. The publisher cannot accept responsibility for ill-health or injury, however caused. Be prepared to summon help in an emergency: see *bit.ly/MR-emergency*

Following the effects of the global pandemic, nobody can predict which of the facilities shown on our mapping and listed on page 7 will survive from 2022 onward. Check for yourself before relying on any.

This route was devised by the authors working from sources identified on page 78 and researched during 2021.   Before setting off, you are advised to check for updates and diversions: *www.rucsacs.com/books/fw1*

Feedback is welcome and will be rewarded

Readers are encouraged to send comments (on the route and/or the book) to **info@rucsacs.com**. All feedback will be acted upon, and anyone whose comments lead to changes will be entitled to claim a free copy of our next edition upon publication.

Contents

Foreword

The 1650s and 1660s were a particularly turbulent time in English history – the Plague, the Fire of London, Cromwell's Lord Protectorship, the restoration of the monarchy and the suppression of religious dissidents are covered on pages 14-16. In these times George Fox became an itinerant preacher, walking up and down the country speaking the truth as he saw it. He paid a heavy price with hardship and eight spells in prison, and, with support from his wife Margaret Fell Fox, he founded the Religious Society of Friends or Quakers: see pages 17-21.

Today, going for a walk is recognised as therapeutic – a good way of clearing the head and sorting out your thoughts. Following a long-distance route with its ever-changing scenery (rather than a familiar, local route) provides great satisfaction – ways found, miles covered, landmarks and turning points achieved.

Being away from your normal routine, your mundane tasks, gives a new perspective on life's issues. It gives you space to sort out your thoughts and helps you to get in touch with your inner self. Walking also lets you discover and recognise new or buried ideas and to consider them quietly, slowly. Then 'full-on' ideas can be allowed to simmer, cure or 'be seasoned' – as Quakers would say.

Many of the paths described here are historic routes, well-trodden by generations past. How was the path for those previous users? They were probably not at leisure, perhaps focussed on the job to be done, but one hopes also able to appreciate mild weather, the sun on distant slopes or the views from high ground.

To paraphrase an Irish blessing: as you walk this route, may the wind be always at your back and may the sun shine warm upon you!

Jocelyn Bell Burnell
University of Oxford

Howgill Fells

1 Planning

George Fox's 1652 journey from Barley to Swarthmoor Hall was our inspiration, but we do not claim to follow his footsteps. We thought long and hard about this issue when developing the route, and we referred often to the Boultons' excellent book *In Fox's Footsteps*: see page 78. To understand why we split the route into two guidebooks, and why we simplified the Boultons' major zigzags, please visit our website: *www.rucsacs.com/books/fw1*.

This guidebook focuses on George Fox's life and his walk as far as Sedbergh, whilst its sequel continues the walk to Swarthmoor Hall: see page 78. At the heart of the latter is Margaret Fell's transition from mistress of Swarthmoor to organiser of the Quakers. Each guidebook describes a walk that visits many sites of key importance in Quaker history and can be completed within one week. We hope that this will introduce some Quakers to long-distance walking and many long-distance walkers to Quakerism.

A note on terminology

The official name of the Quaker movement is the *Religious Society of Friends*. Although *Quaker* was originally coined as a pejorative term, it is now often used interchangeably with *Friend*. In general, Quakers are more likely to refer to each other as *Friends*, whilst non-Quakers are more likely to use the term *Quakers*, especially for clarity in speech – where *Friends* and *friends* sound alike.

Best time of year and weather

Most people will opt to walk this Way in late spring, summer or early autumn. Whitsun week echoes the timing of George Fox's 1652 journey, and wildflowers are at their best in late spring and summer. However, birds are more active and visible during early spring and late autumn. Accommodation will be more limited out of season, so the best times overall are from Easter to October.

In theory, the Way could be walked at any time of year. Its highest point is the summit of Pendle Hill at only 557 m (1830 ft). However, winter walking is always subject to short hours of daylight, greater chance of wet, windy weather and sodden ground in the offroad sections. It's wise to keep checking on the weather forecast as your walk progresses: see page 78.

Unless you are familiar with fairly high latitude (about 54° N) you may be surprised by how short the days can become – fewer than eight daylight hours in late December. To check on sunrise and sunset times in advance, see page 78.

Which direction?

We describe the route from Barley to Sedbergh because that follows Fox's sequence: his vision on Pendle Hill preceded his ramblings around the dales to Firbank Fell near Sedbergh and the Pulpit where he delivered his outdoor sermon. In theory you could walk it in reverse, but we advise against it. You would on trend be walking into the wind, and our text instructions cover the northward direction only, so you'd have to rely on our maps: it's harder than you think to follow directions in 'reverse'.

If you later decide to complete the walk to Swarthmoor Hall, Ulverston, you would resume from Sedbergh anyway. The two day-walks in Sedbergh (see pages 68 to 77) can be done in either order after arrival; or, if you live nearby, either or both could be completed on a separate occasion.

How long will it take?

The overall distance (62 miles/100 km) to Sedbergh is presented in five sections and for many that will be five full days with some early starts. However you can split the route differently to suit your fitness, travel arrangements and accommodation choices. The route is intended as a long and enjoyable walk, not as a test of endurance or speed. For some, the 17 miles/27 km from Sawley to Malham will make too long a day, but it can be split further at Gisburn and/or Hellifield.

Distances are shown in Table 1, in which you will see sections that appear unequal in length but they take account of gradients and terrain, as well as overnight accommodation. Most people will find the 14·7 miles/23·7 km from Far Gearstones to Sedbergh makes an easier day than the shorter distance from Malham to Buckden. And although the two Sedbergh day-walks are both under 10 miles, there is so much Quaker heritage to see, and so many places to spend time reflecting, that each fully justifies an entire day.

Table 1

	miles	km
Barley		
	5·6	9·0
Sawley		
	16·8	27·0
Malham		
	12·5	20·1
Buckden		
	12·4	20·0
Far Gearstones		
	14·7	23·7
Sedbergh		
Cross Keys	9·8	15·8
Quaker Trail	9·4	15·1
Total	**81·2**	**130·7**

Accommodation and refreshments

Many walkers seek a hot evening meal and a soft bed after a hard day's walking. With this in mind, we have split the route in the expectation that you will probably wish to overnight in each of Sawley, Malham, Buckden and Far Gearstones, followed by a couple of nights in Sedbergh. Table 2 shows where you can find accommodation and refreshments, or at least where you could in 2021. In most cases the ticks refer to permanent establishments but we have included selected locations based on *airbnb.co.uk*. The fallout from the Covid 19 pandemic may mean that some options will close and may not reopen. Check carefully before making plans.

As of 2021, a few hostels, bunkhouses and campsites were spread along the route and they too are listed in Table 2. The ultimate low-cost accommodation is a tent that you carry, but this could be very challenging. Official campsites are sparse, especially in the southern part of the route, and you would need to carry heavy loads to include sleeping equipment, cooking gear and food. To undertake this route by camping demands considerable fitness and previous experience.

Refreshments are generally covered by the main overnight stops having at least one pub, café or take-away. If your dietary needs are specialist, or you feel you need frequent snacks, carry your own supplies. However, if you have a hearty breakfast and a good evening meal you may need to carry little extra food. In any event, carry plenty of drinking water for the day's walk, unless you rely on purifying tablets or filters.

Facilities along the Way

	B&B, hotel	hostel, bunkhouse	café, pub	shop	campsite
Barley	✓		✓		
Downham	✓	✓	✓		
Sawley	✓		✓		
*Gisburn**	✓		✓	✓	
Paythorne			✓		
Hellifield	✓		✓	✓	
Kirkby Malham	✓		✓		
Malham	✓		✓	✓	✓
Arncliffe	✓				
*Starbotton**	✓		✓		✓
Buckden	✓	✓	✓	✓	✓
Hubberholme	✓				
Yockenthwaite	✓				
Nethergill	✓				✓
Swarthghyll	✓	✓			
Far Gearstones	✓				
*Ribblehead**	✓	✓			
Cowgill	✓				
Dent Village	✓		✓	✓	✓
Sedbergh	✓		✓	✓	✓
Cautley (Cross Keys)	✓		✓		
Bramaskew Farm	✓				

* places in italics are offroute; B&B may include AirBnB

Pendle Hill from Haw Lane

Navigation, waymarking and experience

The mapping in Part 3 is detailed and closely linked with the route description. If you follow directions carefully, navigation should be straightforward. Distances are shown by mileage markers that are cumulative from Barley, except for the two Sedbergh day-walks which both show distances from St Andrew's Church. Each page also carries a pale grey km grid and north is always straight up the page. The key to map symbols and colours is inside the back cover.

As of 2022 the Friends Way had no dedicated waymarking, and although there are plenty of signs you need to stay alert for which ones you are meant to be following. We offer detailed advice within the text about when to follow – variously – the Pendle Way, Lancashire Way, Ribble Way, Pennine Bridleway, Pennine Way and Dales Way. The photos above give you some idea of the variety of signs to look out for. But you also need to be vigilant about when to stop following certain signs. On occasions you have to look for an obscure arrow or detect which gate or stile to aim at, or try to follow a trod path.

If you have never attempted a long-distance walk before, we encourage you to obtain and study our *Notes for novices* (see page 78). We suggest that you don't go alone, especially not in winter or when poor visibility means that map and compass skills may be needed. Having said that, if you take time to prepare and plan your expedition, this could be a very suitable choice for your first long walk and an ideal preparation for the follow-on walk to Swarthmoor Hall.

North towards the Three Peaks in winter

Getting there and away

Barley is about 30 miles north of Manchester, nearly 40 miles west of Leeds and under 30 miles north-east of Preston. To reach it by public transport you need to use at least one bus and probably a combination of buses and train. From Manchester Victoria, take a train (Northern Rail, roughly hourly, duration 75 minutes) to Clitheroe, then a Rossendale Transport 66 or 67 bus (roughly hourly, duration 40 minutes) to Barley. This combination takes nearly 3 hours but could be done inside an hour if a car or taxi is an option for the 31 miles by road. The nearest airport is Manchester, 10 miles south of the city centre: frequent trains reach Manchester (Piccadilly) within 20 minutes.

From Preston take a train to Nelson (departs roughly hourly, duration one hour) then a Rossendale 66 or 67 bus (roughly hourly, duration 25 minutes) to Barley. Alternatively (usually cheaper) take a Stagecoach bus 280 from Preston to Clitheroe (roughly two-hourly, duration 50 minutes) then the Rossendale 66 or 67 bus (roughly hourly, duration 40 minutes) to Barley.

From London, it can take six hours to reach Barley using two trains and two buses: LNER train from King's Cross to Leeds, then LNER or Northern Rail to Keighley. From Keighley take a Transdev M4 bus to Nelson and finally a Rossendale 66 or 67 bus to Barley. As above, using a car or taxi will speed up the last section of the journey.

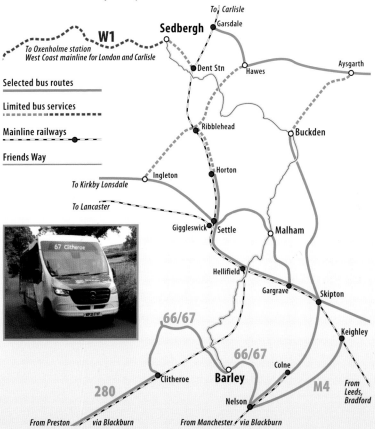

9

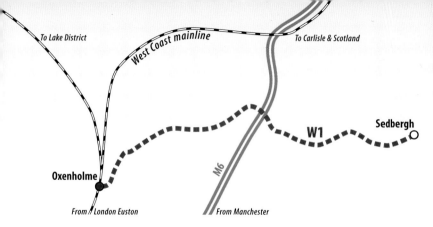

To return from Sedbergh, most people will use the nearest railway station – Oxenholme, 10 miles to the west. Woofs of Sedbergh (*woofsofsedbergh.co.uk*) operate a W1 bus to Oxenholme but currently only once a day on weekdays, so a taxi would connect with trains much more flexibly. Oxenholme is on the west coast mainline and direct trains from London Euston take less than three hours (Avanti West Coast via Preston). Heading north, trains to Glasgow Central via Carlisle can take as little as 2 hours with Avanti West Coast, slightly longer by Transpennine Express.

For Manchester, again reach Oxenholme by bus or taxi and use the hourly train (Transpennine Express) for a fast and direct journey time of just 65-70 minutes. Northern Rail also has services, but they are less frequent, take a bit longer and you may have to change at Lancaster or Preston.

If you are seeking to complete this route in several trips, let alone as day-walks, be warned: rural public transport was both sparse and infrequent even before the pandemic and you would need to study the timetables carefully and check before relying on them. Consult the splendid network provided by DalesBus, which links places such as Dent with Sedbergh and Cautley, but some of these are on certain days of the week or perhaps on summer Sundays only: see page 78 for details.

Terrain and gradients

The Way runs over a wide variety of surfaces, ranging from grassy footpaths and farm tracks to limestone pavement, stone steps and tarmac roads or pavements. The photos give some idea of the range of surfaces, but be aware that rainfall (not only during your walk but also before it) also affects offroad surfaces and can make for slow going.

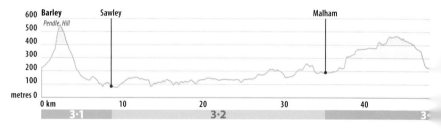

Some sections of the route have a number of gates and stiles, and you may be surprised by how much these small obstacles reduce your average speed. They present extra challenges if you are walking with a dog. Even flights of steps and footbridges may slow you more than you expect. Many of the paths are fairly well-drained, but your footwear needs to be waterproof for walking in the rain and through long wet grass.

The route begins with a stiff climb up Pendle Hill to 557 m (1830 ft) followed by a steepish descent, but the next 20 miles or so is relatively low-level (but far from flat) until the ascent to the top of Malham Cove by 400 stone steps. From Malham Tarn there are two notable climbs (to 450 m and 520 m) in order to reach Wharfedale. The Dales Way then heads up relatively gradually to another high point of just over 520 m/1705 ft on Cam High Road before a long slow descending approach to Sedbergh (about 110 m).

How tiring a day feels often depends more on smaller undulations and frequency of stiles than the maximum height above sea level. However it's useful to be aware of the altitudes involved, especially if the weather forecast predicts low cloud. Navigation in poor visibility requires skill and experience with map and compass.

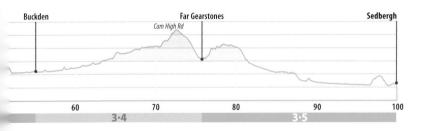

Buckden   Far Gearstones   Sedbergh

Cam High Rd

60   70   80   90   100

3·4   3·5

Responsible access

England has four categories of public rights of way: footpaths (walkers and wheelchairs/mobility scooters only), bridleways (walkers, cyclists, horseriders and wheelchairs/ mobility scooters) and two kinds of byway – restricted (no motor vehicles) or byway open to all traffic (BOAT).

Rights of way are marked on Ordnance Survey and other maps, and recent maps also show areas of Access Land that allow walkers to escape from paths under agreements reached with the landowners. Restrictions are explained at *www.openaccess.gov.uk*. In summary, in England you have no automatic right to walk over, let alone camp upon, privately owned land.

Countryside Code

Respect other people
- Consider the local community and other people enjoying the outdoors
- Park carefully so access to gateways and driveways is clear
- Leave gates and property as you find them
- Follow paths but give way to others where it's narrow

Protect the natural environment
- Leave no trace of your visit, take all your litter home
- Don't have BBQs or fires
- Keep dogs under effective control
- Dog poo – bag it and bin it –

Enjoy the outdoors
- Plan ahead, check what facilities are open, be prepared
- Follow advice and local signs and obey social distancing measures

Throughout this guidebook, we have been careful to direct you along footpaths, bridleways and Access Land. As you walk, be guided by the 2021 version of the Countryside Code.

Livestock, walkers and dogs

Much of the Way passes through farmland and moorland with livestock. There may be cattle or sheep grazing near the path or even standing or lying across it. Approach cattle with caution, especially if there are calves around. Most difficulties can be avoided by giving them a wide berth, staying alert to their body language and never approaching pregnant animals, let alone those with young.

If you walk with a dog, it must be under close control, always within sight. Between 1 March and 31 July legally dogs must be on a lead when on Open Access Land. During lambing time (from February/March until June) your dog will be unwelcome in any fields with sheep. During the same season birds may be nesting on the ground, and again dogs must be under very close control. If cattle react aggressively to your dog, let go of it immediately and take the safest route out of the field.

Local words, placenames and pronunciation

Many words in common use in the dales derive from Old Norse, the language of the Vikings who arrived here in the ninth century. Understanding their meanings may help with decoding some placenames.

beck	stream	laithe	stone barn
combe	hillside hollow	moor	upland, often heather-clad
dale	valley	rigg	ridge
fell	hill, high moor	scar	cliff
force/foss	waterfall	snout/spout	waterfall resembling a nose
gill/ghyll	ravine, mountain stream	tarn	upland or mountain lake
ginnel	narrow passage between buildings		

The pronunciation of some placenames may be unexpected and we have tried to indicate these below: put stress on the syllable in **bold**

Hubberholme **hub**-bram	Malham **mall**-em
Kirkby **kerr**-bee	Oughtershaw **out**-er-shaw
Lea Yeat lee yatt	Sedbergh sed-ber or **seb**-ber

Packing checklist

What you need to bring with you depends both on your personal needs and also on your itinerary and the season and likely weather. If you are tackling the Way in sections, or if you have access to a support vehicle at any time, you may be able to carry few overnight things. If you are carrying everything for yourself, be aware that every kilogram counts. A heavy rucksack will not only make harder work out of stiles and steep slopes, it will also take longer to pack and unpack. Travel light and enjoy the walk.

Experienced walkers will already know what they habitually need, and may differ about what is essential and desirable. Novices may find the following checklist helpful:

Essential

- comfortable, waterproof walking boots
- specialist walking socks
- breathable clothing in layers
- waterproof jacket and over-trousers
- hat and gloves
- guidebook, map and compass
- in case of injury, whistle and torch for attracting attention
- water carrier and plenty of water (or purification tablets/filter)
- enough food to last between supply points
- first aid kit including blister treatment
- toiletries and overnight necessities
- insect repellent and sun protection (summer)
- rucksack (at least 35 litres)
- waterproof rucksack cover or liner, e.g. bin (garbage) bag.

Cash machines are sparse along the Way but credit/debit cards are widely accepted. Bin (garbage) bags have many uses e.g. store wet clothing or prevent hypothermia.

Desirable

- walking pole(s)
- binoculars: useful for navigation and spotting wildlife
- camera (ideally light and rugged), also spare batteries and memory cards
- pouch or secure pockets, to keep small items handy but safe
- gaiters (to keep mud and water out of boots)
- toilet tissue (biodegradable)
- small plastic bags for litter
- spare socks: changing socks at lunchtime can relieve damp feet
- spare shoes (e.g. trainers, crocs or sandals)
- towel if hostelling
- notebook and pen
- smartphone (cellphone): useful for arrangements **but don't rely on one for emergencies**.

Camping

If you are camping, you need much more gear, including tent, sleeping gear, camping stove, fuel, cooking utensils and food. Your rucksack will need to be larger e.g. 50-80 litres, and camping could add 5-10 kg to its weight. Previous experience is advisable.

2·1 England in the 17th century

England in the time of the civil wars and their aftermath was a hothouse of ideas. Some, such as the panic about witches, now seem a brutal throwback to a more superstitious age. The endless religious disputes have long since lost their intensity. However, new political ideas from this era are recognisable as foundations of the modern age.

During much of the 17th century, England appeared violent and ungovernable. There were several civil wars (during the 1640s and later), one king was executed for treason (1649) and another forcibly deposed and exiled (1688). Most of these events involved Scotland – with which England had shared a king since 1603. However the two countries remained separate until the union of their parliaments in 1707.

Witchcraft

There had been a fear of witches with supernatural powers since ancient times, but persecution had been relatively rare. The Inquisitions set up by the Catholic Church were generally sceptical about claims of witchcraft. By the late 15th century the climate was changing, with witchcraft becoming associated with devil-worship and heresy. The Reformation and subsequent religious wars intensified the fears.

In 1612 twelve people from the area around Pendle Hill – two men and ten women – were accused of ten murders using witchcraft. Following trials at Lancaster and York, ten were executed by hanging, one was found not guilty and one died in prison. One of the women, Alice Nutter, came from a wealthy family but was found guilty and hanged on 20 August 1612. In 2012 she was commemorated by a statue in Roughlee, just a couple of miles from Barley.

The star witness at the trials was a nine year-old child, and dubious accusations were made of child murder, cannibalism and witches being visited by Satan. The accused were not allowed to call witnesses and were denied access to lawyers. In fact the trials were motivated by fears of the survival of Catholicism in this remote area, and a desire to please the king, James I, whose background in Presbyterian Scotland had given him a morbid interest in witchcraft.

The civil war saw widespread witch-hunting in territory controlled by Parliament. Matthew Hopkins, who described himself as Witchfinder General, was responsible for securing 300 convictions for witchcraft in the years 1644-47.

In the later 17th century accusations of witchcraft continued, both against George Fox and also made by him against some Cockermouth 'wicked women' in 1653. The last executions in England were at Exeter in 1682, although Scotland persisted until 1727. Bizarrely, the Witchcraft Act was still being used to prosecute spiritualists and fortune-tellers until its repeal in 1951.

Statue of Alice Nutter, Roughlee

Religious background

Religious upheaval was a feature of 16th century England. Henry VIII had started his reign by defending the Catholic Church against all forms of heresy. After the Pope refused to sanction his divorce, Henry broke away and proclaimed himself head of the church in England. However, his beliefs remained largely unchanged, and England became the only country whose citizens could be prosecuted for being either a Catholic or a supporter of the Protestant Reformation.

After a period of Protestantism under Edward VI and a reversion to Catholicism under Mary I, the next monarch Elizabeth I established a kind of broad church solution in which many forms of Protestant worship were permitted. Catholics, however, continued to be persecuted.

In 1603, when James VI, King of Scotland, became also James I of England, many stricter Protestants in England hoped that he might bring Presbyterian worship from Scotland, but their hopes were dashed. James and his son, Charles I, became committed to the idea of a fully united kingdom of England & Wales, Scotland and Ireland and of a national church based on

high church principles. There was widespread protest in Scotland when an attempt was made to impose an English-style prayer book. The mass signing of the National Covenant in Greyfriars Churchyard, Edinburgh, in 1638 turned out to be the first step towards a rising against Charles.

Charles' high-church religious policies were equally unpopular among some English people who objected to the idea of any kind of established, state-backed church and rejected the authority of bishops. These included Presbyterians, Puritans and Independents, who favoured simple forms of worship and a strict moral code.

Thousands queued to sign the Covenant

Civil wars

Religious differences were not the only cause of the civil wars. Charles's extravagance created a need to impose new taxes. This, in turn, required the consent of Parliament. Charles called a new Parliament in 1628 but it imposed conditions before allowing him to levy taxes. Charles then ruled without Parliament for a decade but his actions were limited by lack of money. Opposition to his concept of the divine right of kings steadily grew as more democratic ideas spread.

In 1640 Charles was twice obliged to turn again to Parliament. The first one was quickly dismissed, but a second remained in place until dissolved by Oliver Cromwell in 1653 and passed legislation limiting the power of the king.

An attempt by Charles to arrest five of its members in 1642 led to war. Fighting was inconclusive during the first three years but, after the Battle of Naseby in 1645, victory for the Parliamentary forces became inevitable. In 1646 Charles was taken prisoner by the Scots and handed over to the English Parliament.

Oliver Cromwell, from an engraving post-1800

Between 1646 and 1648, Royalists, Parliamentary Presbyterians and the New Model Army contended for influence but without a decisive outcome. In 1648 the Scots invaded England on the basis of a promise from Charles to establish Presbyterianism in England within three years. By the middle of the year, the Army led by Fairfax and Cromwell had achieved victory. They purged Parliament of all but the Independents. Citing the various secret pacts that Charles had concluded, most importantly with the Scots, Parliament then put him on trial for treason. Charles was executed on 30 January 1649.

Political and religious challenge

The mid-17th century saw an extraordinary flowering of political and religious thought. An important strand of new political thinking was that of the Levellers. They believed in extending the vote to all men, equality before the law and religious tolerance. They were highly influential in the years 1645-48 but later lost ground to the leaders of the New Model Army, particularly Oliver Cromwell (1599-1658). Nevertheless, their ideas were of lasting significance. The origins of the late-18th century American and French Revolutions are easily traced to the views of the Levellers.

Other groups were motivated more by religious considerations. The Seekers, founded around 1620 by the three Legate brothers, considered all organised churches to be corrupt. The Ranters, who were strong during the Commonwealth period, held a similar view. They had no central organisation or leader and denied the authority of all churches and scripture, advising people to listen to the divine within themselves.

One of the most important new groups to emerge in this period was the Society of Friends or Quakers. They shared with Seekers and Ranters the belief that contact with God should be direct, not mediated by a separate priesthood. In the 1650s they clashed with the authorities because they rejected social hierarchies and religious conventions. They held public meetings for worship, without fixed orders of service, at which both women and men preached. Later they became known for their plain dress, commitment to non-violence, opposition to slavery and their commitment to greater equality for women. Their founder, George Fox, preached widely that God is within us all and he rejected the need for ordained priests. His role in challenging religious authority and uniting dissident groups is described in the next section.

2·2 George Fox and Quakerism

This book celebrates Fox's journey that led to the foundation of the Quaker movement. His looks were striking – tall and broad, he had long hair and was seldom seen without his hat, which he would wear in church to signal his dissidence.

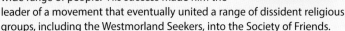

During May and June 1652 he preached while travelling through Lancashire, Yorkshire and Westmorland, gathering support from a wide range of people. His success made him the leader of a movement that eventually united a range of dissident religious groups, including the Westmorland Seekers, into the Society of Friends.

Although George had preached in Leicestershire earlier, his seminal journey in 1652 began on Pendle Hill and continued north through Downham and Malham to the Yorkshire Dales and Sedbergh. Over the next few weeks he continued into what was then Lancashire and arrived at Swarthmoor Hall, near Ulverston. There his preaching made a deep impression on the Fell household and their friends. Among those who were converted was Margaret Fell, then the wife of Thomas Fell and mistress of Swarthmoor Hall.

Thomas Fell became a Justice of the Peace in 1641 and a member of the Long Parliament four years later. Fox's ministry had impressed him too, although he never publicly declared himself a Quaker. He was at least a closet supporter, and until his death in 1658 he often protected Fox and other Quakers from persecution.

Early life

Born in July 1624 in Fenny Drayton, George was the son of a Leicestershire weaver. The family was fairly prosperous and George was apprenticed to a local tradesman by the age of 12. His parents were Puritan and George had studied the Bible closely, and in his autobiography he claims that he already 'knew pureness and righteousness' as a child.

However, he was restless and troubled, and aged 19 he left home 'to seek the truth'. His own ideas were radical, and he challenged not only priesthood but also the system of tithes that supported the church and even the churches themselves – buildings that he dismissed as 'steeplehouses'. He proclaimed his beliefs at every opportunity, and was soon in trouble with the authorities. His first spell in prison was in Nottingham in 1649 for blasphemy.

In 1651 he refused a captaincy in the New Model Army, preferring to remain in gaol, because he believed in 'the virtue of that life and power that took away the occasion for all wars'. When he set off for Pendle Hill the following year, he was only 27 years old but already a supremely confident preacher and experienced evangelist. He was utterly convinced of his unique relationship with God and his personal ability to transmit his Truth. Although his leadership was contested later in life, his charisma and conviction lent a powerful momentum to the early day of Quakerism.

Pendle Hill

Journey in 1652

He started from Pendle Hill and was 'moved by the Lord to go atop of it' where he had his vision of 'a great people to be gathered'. Gazing at the distant hills to the north he saw fertile ground for his message to take root, and to the west he saw the inspiring gleam of light on the 'Lancashire Sea' – Morecambe Bay, near his journey's end at Ulverston. 'The Lord let me see atop of the hill in what places he had a great people'. Later he had a further vision that evoked the Book of Revelation: 'the Lord ... let me see a great people in white raiment by a river's side coming to the Lord'. At his alehouse lodgings that night, he told all this to his landlady who urged him to write it down. She then had it copied and spread it through the countryside, helping to build Fox's gathering momentum.

Soon afterwards in Sedbergh, having climbed high near a yew tree in order to make himself heard, Fox preached for hours to a large crowd outside St Andrew's Church. His audience was apparently spellbound, and included several Seeker leaders who invited him to join them at their rally to be held on nearby Firbank Fell on 13 June. By this time, word had spread about the charismatic preacher and families arrived from all directions, making a crowd of over 1000.

Fox's Pulpit

In the morning of 13 June, Seekers Francis Howgill and John Audland preached, both hoping that George Fox would reinforce and focus their message. After everyone else had lunched, George (who drank only some water) climbed up to a dramatic crag now known as Fox's Pulpit. With all eyes now turned on him, he preached fluently and passionately for three hours, demanding the end of the false church with its hireling priests, steeplehouses and tithes. Fox was convinced that the time had come to restore the true Christian Church, to open hearts and minds to the inner light and to recognise the divine truth.

Persecution and imprisonment

Despite continuing controversies and sporadic local persecution, Quakerism grew rapidly throughout England in the 1650s. The restoration of the monarchy in 1660 marked the beginning of a period of persecution for nonconformist groups, and Quakers were viewed with particular suspicion. This was enshrined in law by the Quaker Act of 1662 and the Conventicle Acts of 1664 and 1670 that banned all religious services except those of the Church of England.

Conditions in prison were harsh, with unpalatable food in pitiful quantities, extreme cold and damp and polluted air. Quakers were typically stoical and they often impressed their fellow prisoners and sometimes their gaolers as sincere prisoners of conscience.

Imprisoned in a foul smoky tower in Lancaster prison in 1664, Fox did not complain, instead embarking on what became his *Short Journal*. Severely crippled by arthritis, he was dragged from his tower room and forced to ride to Scarborough Castle where he was imprisoned in appalling conditions.

Scarborough Castle (12th century keep)

'A threepenny loaf served me three weeks and sometimes longer' he reported. Its location on sea cliffs ensured that his quarters were cold and damp, exacerbating the pain in his joints. Cruellest of all, he was not allowed any visitors, although many Friends came to the castle gate.

Fox set a shining example of conducting himself bravely and with dignity. Quaker behaviour outside prison was also admired, especially in London where the bubonic plague (Black Death) killed about 20% of the population and caused many wealthier citizens to flee, including Anglican priests who abandoned their parishioners. Quakers from all over England sent funds, and brave Friends defied the law to visit Newgate Gaol and the guarded homes of sick Quakers. Quaker money was used to smuggle food through the windows of houses sealed by the plague.

Finally released from Scarborough in August 1666, Fox had been a prisoner of conscience for nearly three years, much of it spent in solitary confinement. Unbroken and uncowed, he worked to establish a structure of local, regional and national organisation for the Quaker movement, in which women took part in decision-making and exercised authority alongside men. In early 1669 he travelled to Ireland and was energised by the Irish Quakers' support.

Marriage to Margaret Fell

During his time in Ireland, George somehow 'sensed a divine command' that he should marry Margaret Fell who had been his good friend and strongest supporter for 17 years. Margaret had been widowed some 11 years ago, and had been an active and effective Quaker since 1652. She was becoming the movement's chief organiser and published many epistles. After consulting their families and friends, they were married in Bristol on 27 October 1669.

It was – to say the least – an unusual marriage. Not only was she ten years older than him, but also his superior in social class and wealth. George was scrupulous about making no claim on Margaret's estate, again contrary to the custom of the times. Almost throughout the marriage, their Quaker work took precedence over spending time together. Just ten days after the wedding, they set off northward from Bristol and parted company after just a couple of hours: George reported 'I passed on ... in the work of the Lord into Wiltshire', while his bride travelled on alone to Swarthmoor, her lifelong home.

Working separately for the Quaker cause became the norm throughout their marriage – George mainly in London and Margaret at Swarthmoor. Her estate had passed to the children of her first marriage, and her seven daughters supported George warmly and welcomed him as stepfather. However, of the 22 years that their marriage lasted, George spent less than five years at Swarthmoor, most of that time recovering from ill health and imprisonment. Once restored to health, he would set off again to spread the word.

Despite the rigours of long journeys in those days and her greater age, Margaret had to do nearly all the travelling to see George. She was 76 when she made her ninth trip to London to see him in 1690.

Travels and later years

In August 1671 George set sail for Barbados to spread the Quaker message, enduring a voyage during which he became very unwell. Upon arrival he spent nearly three weeks bedridden and fasting. In 1672 he moved on to Jamaica and sailed through stormy weather to Maryland, Virginia and Carolina. He set up new Meetings, attracted attention from 'men and women of account' and preached successfully to native Americans. He also worked hard to try to reconcile factions within the movement. It would have been a gruelling trip for a young person in good health.

He returned to find he was too late to see his mother before she died in Fenny Drayton, and he was soon imprisoned at Worcester – his eighth incarceration. Finally released after 14 months in 1675, he suffered terrible ill health, but his work and travels were far from finished. He took his mission to Holland and Germany in 1677 with William Penn, and displayed immense physical courage in managing horses at a swollen river crossing near Lüneburg. The more challenging the journey, the more he seemed energised.

Finally he returned to Swarthmoor in 1678 for a period of recuperation. His last decade was spent mainly in London, writing his *Journal* and epistles to Friends. His last contact with Margaret was in 1690 when she visited him from spring until June. After further travels, George returned to London in January 1691 and fell ill with a mysterious 'cold strike to the heart'. After three days in bed, he died a serene death. His coffin was carried through the London streets to the dissenters' burial ground at Bunhill Fields, followed by 4000 Quakers.

Fox's gravestone, Bunhill Fields

Fox's legacy

George Fox endured enormous hardships throughout his life and was persecuted for his beliefs. Near the end of his life, he saw William of Orange and Mary Stuart invited to rule England as joint monarchs in 1689. This led directly to the Act of Toleration that granted freedom of worship to all Protestant Nonconformists. It marked the end of persecution and a major step towards freedom of conscience – a fitting tribute to George Fox and the movement he had founded.

For all that his marriage was largely maintained at a distance, it was extremely important to the foundation of his movement. His leadership would never have been as effective without the lifelong efforts of his wife Margaret Fell Fox. If he was the father of Quakerism, she was its mother. She was an indefatigable organiser, letter-writer and advocate for George's ideas and she too spent time in prison. She also lived and worked much longer than he, and had established her home, Swarthmoor Hall, as the headquarters of Quakerism in the north. To do her justice, we dedicate our successor guidebook to her: see page 78.

Finally, in addition to its role in creating freedom of conscience, Quakerism has also created an architectural legacy. Quakers believe that worship does not require a special building, and indeed Fox was happy to preach outdoors in order to avoid 'steeplehouses' - his dismissive term for traditional churches. However, practical considerations soon meant that meetinghouses were needed – some adapted from existing buildings, others purpose built.

The hallmarks of a meetinghouse are simplicity, community and equality, with a total absence of traditional liturgical objects and symbols. Brigflatts is a superb example, built during Fox's lifetime in 1675, and the oldest meetinghouse in the north of England. Many of its original oak furnishings survive intact, and its simple benches and gallery make a tranquil space for Quakers to meet and share their faith. Our route visits it on page 72 and it is pleasing to know that it is still in regular use by local Friends for their meetings. It is a perfect place to sit and contemplate the lives and legacy of George and Margaret Fox.

Brigflatts Meetinghouse, near Sedbergh

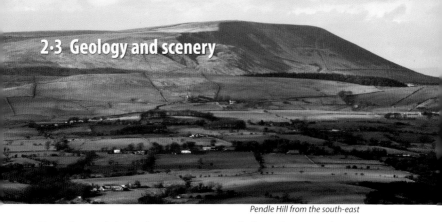

2·3 Geology and scenery

Pendle Hill from the south-east

To understand the landscapes that you walk through, start with an image of their formation. Imagine the deep clear tropical sea of long ago – about 360 million years ago (MYA). Near its surface, minute plankton lived and died. Their shells fell to the sea bed and were compacted to form limestone.

Later, river deltas advanced, depositing thick layers of sand. As the shore advanced, coastal lagoons formed and dense forests grew up. Trees fell into the stagnant water and accumulated in thick layers among the shale, clay and sands. Heat, pressure and time produce seams of coal, and the period from about 360-300 MYA when coalfields were formed is known as *carboniferous*.

About 250 MYA, deep within the molten earth, convection currents carried the continent that became the Americas to collide with the continent which became Europe and Asia. Ripples formed on the edge of the collision zone, like an ill-fitting carpet. One such ripple formed a north-south ridge in what is now northern England – known as the Pennines, England's backbone of hills: see the map opposite.

The coal-bearing measures then formed outcrops on either side of the Pennines and the coalfields supported the industrialisation of urban parts of Lancashire and Yorkshire. Before the coal was extracted, these measures lay on top of the *gritstone* – a variety of coarse-grained sandstone that was compressed and hardened while subject to pressure and dissolved minerals. Gritstone is sometimes called *millstone grit* because of its use in millstones. Where the gritstone has been eroded, the underlying limestone is exposed.

Our walk starts from Pendle Hill in the mid-Pennines and extends to the Howgill Fells, a group of hills north of Sedbergh that form a westward extension of the Pennines. Pendle Hill is a remnant of the gritstone which once arched over the whole of the Pennines. Erosion of the underlying limestone went on until it undercut the eastern edge, leaving a steep scarp face of exposed gritstone. You may notice the similarity of shape of Pendle with each of the taller Three Peaks (see page 58): all were formed in a similar way.

Lancashire

Coal measures   Gritstone   Shale   Limestone

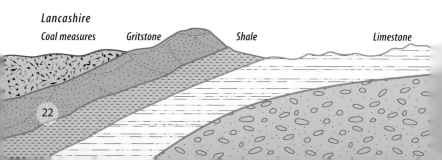

Scarp faces on Ingleborough

A lot has happened since the mountain-building period about 250 MYA. Further periods of deposition, largely of chalk, were followed by another major buckling of the crust. This was when Africa moved towards Europe about 50 MYA, during the Alpine mountain-building period.

More recently and dramatically, from about 2 MYA until about 10,000 years ago, various Ice Ages prevailed. In the last of these, a deep sheet of ice covered the whole of northern England. As it inched southwards, it cut deep broad U-shaped valleys and left deposits of sand, gravel, and clay containing boulders. Ice typically filled the whole of the valley and slowly scoured its walls as well as its floor. The end result was neither the V-shaped river valley typical of gritstone, nor the flat wide valleys found in soft sedimentary clays, but a pronounced U-shape. You walk through Wharfedale, which is a fine example.

Limestone creates a very different landscape. The atmosphere contains carbon dioxide that partly dissolves in rainwater, making very dilute carbonic acid. Limestone is a hard rock that can be 'dressed' (polished) to a smooth surface, widely used for public buildings, cathedrals and viaducts. The dark limestone of Dentdale is known as Dent Marble and was used for Dent Head and Arten Gill Viaducts: see page 60.

Yorkshire

Limestone   Shale   Gritstone   Coal measures

Older rocks

23

Limestone pavement above Malham Cove

When puddles of rainwater form on the surface of the rock, the carbonic acid seeks out any cracks and eats into them, creating deep fissures. Once they become deep enough, the fissures collect moss, grass and wildflowers; eventually even shrubs may take root. Flat topped blocks of limestone known as clints are separated by deep grykes (grikes). You walk across an impressive example over the top of Malham Cove. Where the clints are fairly flat and uniform and the grykes straight, the overall effect resembles man-made pavement.

Limestone scenery has distinctive drainage. Water from the surface can dissolve weaknesses in the rock, allowing streams to disappear underground in passages, or to create a network of sunken streams. In places, impressive caverns and caves can form in limestone, with stalagmites and stalactites and cascades. Ingleborough Cave is a popular example.

When you walk through the 'dry valley' Watlowes (see page 48) you are in a limestone gorge created about ten thousand years ago when a huge volume of frozen water was trapped here. Only after the climate became warmer and drier could it sink through the limestone to make the valley dry. (It can flood on occasion, but only after exceptionally prolonged heavy rain.)

The Way through Watlowes, a dry limestone gorge

West over Cautley Crags, near the highest part of the Howgills

Just north of Malham you reach the amazing amphitheatre of Malham Cove with its 70-metre (230 ft) cliffs: see pages 24 and 47. Originally formed along the Middle Craven Fault, the limestone has been eroded by the action of water and ice over millions of years. The huge waterfall that used to drop down its cliffs is no more. Nowadays the water instead sinks into the ground near Malham Tarn and emerges at the foot of these cliffs further south.

It is very unusual to see a lake in limestone country because surface water usually seeps underground, but Malham Tarn is a very fine exception. During the last Ice Age, ice scooped out and filled this large hollow. After the climate warmed, the meltwater could not sink underground because the ice sheet had deposited a layer of glacial clay and debris. This was impermeable, so a lake formed with a depth of up to 4·4 m (14 ft). The Way passes its outflow at mile 25·3, just north of where it goes underground at Watersinks car park.

Further north, around Barth Bridge (mile 57·6), you cross the Dent Fault and the walk continues over much older bedrock – mudstones and sandstones formed more than 400 MYA. After you emerge from Dentdale, start to see the Howgill Fells north of Sedbergh – mainly gritstone. The walk on page 68 takes you towards Cautley Crags: see the photo above.

Yorkshire Dales National Park (YDNP)

The Yorkshire Dales forms one of 15 National Parks recognised by the UK government, designated in 1954 for its natural beauty, diversity of habitats and rich heritage. In its landscapes, geology is made visible and tangible. As well as a working environment that includes over 1000 farms, the Park is also home to 24,000 people. It was extended in 2016 to include parts of Cumbria and a spot of Lancashire, and occupies over 850 square miles (2200 sq km): see *www.yorkshiredales.org.uk*.

The Way enters the National Park just north of Hellifield and remains inside it all the way to Sedbergh and beyond. The Park has five visitor centres, and the Way passes one just as you arrive in Malham: see page 46. It is staffed by helpful and knowledgeable people, there are displays, publications, toilet facilities and a picnic area. For details of its opening times and more, phone 01729 833 200 or visit its web page *bit.ly/YDNP-M*.

2·4 Habitats and wildlife

The Way goes through five main types of habitat:

- rivers, streams and Malham Tarn
- woodland • hay meadow
- limestone pavement and grassland
- heath and moorland

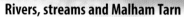

Rivers, streams and Malham Tarn

Grey wagtail

The main rivers that you walk beside are the Ribble, Aire, Wharfe, Dee, Rawthey and Lune, and they have many small tributaries which support similar species.

Waterways and their banks act as corridors for wildlife, as well as making homes and feeding grounds for insects, birds and small mammals. The larger rivers are home to a wide range of fish including trout.

Recognise various kinds of wagtail by their distinctive bobbing movements – especially the pied (black-and-white) and the less common grey wagtail, which has lemon yellow underparts. Look out for the charming dipper, a

Kingfisher

small dark-brown bird with a smart white breast, skilful at collecting larvae and insects from fast-moving streams. If you are lucky enough to spot the turquoise flash of a low-flying tiny bird above a stream, it will be a kingfisher. They prey on aquatic insects and small fish, and are a sign of a high-quality watercourse.

At about 380 m (1250 ft), Malham Tarn is the highest limestone lake in Britain; see page 25 for its formation. Together with its surrounding area, it forms a National Nature Reserve (NNR) and is also part of a much larger Site of Special Scientific Interest. Its raised bog area (Tarn Moss) supports a wide diversity of flora including rare species such as bog rosemary, frog orchid and the carnivorous sundew – shown here consuming an insect trapped in its sticky tentacles.

Common sundew devouring an insect

Otter on river bank

The Tarn itself supports six fish species and various crustaceans, including the white-clawed crayfish. This is Britain's only native crayfish and a key indicator of good water quality. The abundant fish life and protected environment of the tarn has attracted resident otters.

The NNR attracts a huge range of insects and birds, with 157 bird species recorded within a 5-mile radius. Wading birds such as redshanks, curlews, lapwings and oystercatchers can be seen around the tarn's shores and nearby. On the water itself, you may see many kinds of ducks – teal, tufted duck, fish-eating goosander and various kinds of grebe; this is one of the highest breeding areas for the great crested grebe.

Great crested grebe

Woodland and hedgerow

Most of the woodland on the Way stands in its southern, low-lying part, though you go through some patches of woodland (mainly replanted) in Dentdale. Trees are relatively scarce in the Yorkshire Dales and semi-natural ancient woodlands account for only 1% of its entire area. However, they are very important for biodiversity and conservation.

Many birds and small mammals thrive in woodland, and there is encouraging news of the charming red squirrel which is threatened by its larger, non-native grey cousin. Greys not only compete for food, but also carry the squirrelpox disease which is fatal to reds. The Dales is one of very few areas in England where reds may be seen, and recent monitoring suggests that they are holding their ground and perhaps extending their range. The National Park has named them as a priority species for conservation.

Red squirrel

Although fields in the Dales are often thought of as marked out by drystone walls, in several places along the Way (Malhamdale, upper Wharfedale and Dentdale) hedgerows more commonly form the boundaries.

Thorny species such as hawthorn and blackthorn make the traditional barrier to livestock, and also provide support and shelter to softer plants such as hazel, bramble and dog rose. Woodland plants can also flourish, such as ramsons (wild garlic), herb Robert, wood anemone and primrose.

Hay meadow

Swaledale ram

The valley floors and slopes are home to hay meadows that provide feed for livestock including the round-horned Swaledale sheep. These hardy animals really deserve their iconic status – see the YDNP logo on page 25. Swaledales, although domesticated, form part of the quintessential Dales landscape of drystone walls bounding fields of grazing sheep, with stone barns.

In summer, especially in June or July, hay meadows are a haven for wildflowers, fescues and other grasses – up to 120 different species per field. This makes hay meadows of national importance for biodiversity. Bumblebees, butterflies and many other pollinators flourish here, as do small mammals and brown hares. Along the route, the best areas to enjoy this habitat are in Wharfedale, Langstrothdale and Dentdale.

In lowland hay meadows you will often see common knapweed, an excellent pollinator, and yellow rattle, which is semi-parasitic on grass roots and thus helps to prevent vigorous grasses and clovers from driving out wildflowers. Rarer examples include several kinds of orchid. Upland hay meadows are found in Ribblesdale and feature sweet vernal-grass, wood cranesbill and lady's mantle, with rarer species again including many interesting orchids.

Brown hare

Hay meadow with wood cranesbill and buttercup

Limestone pavement and grassland

The formation of limestone pavement is explained on page 24, and the Way passes over a wonderful section at the top of Malham Cove. Look out for wildflowers and unusual ferns growing in the shelter of the grykes. Herb Robert is a wild geranium captured here in a gryke above Malham Cove in October. You may also see a range of delicate ferns, spleenworts and other plants nestling in grykes.

Herb Robert sheltering in a gryke

Since 1993, the limestone cliffs of Malham Cove have been home to a pair of nesting peregrine falcons which you might spot during summer months. Peregrines are powerful, agile falcons that prey on pigeons and other birds that they catch 'on the wing'. They are the world's fastest bird by far, diving at speeds of well over 180 mph (290 kph). To allow it to breathe at such high speeds, it has special baffles in its nostrils.

Of the many small mammals in the Dales, the stoat is one of the most impressive. Larger than its cousin the weasel, it not only preys on small rodents but can easily kill an adult rabbit which is much heavier than itself. Active year-round, they are easiest to spot in the open by their black-tipped tails and distinctive arched-back running. They can be seen bounding across the grass to hide in a drystone wall. On high ground in winter, their coats may turn white for camouflage against the snow.

Stoat

Peregrine falcon

Red grouse

Meadow pipit

Heather moorland occurs on higher ground, typically on thin soils over gritstone, not on limestone. Both heather and bilberry flourish together on acidic soils, and in late July and August the heather carpets the moorland in purple. You will find good examples above Wharfedale at around miles 31-32 and on Blea Moor at about miles 48-9.

Heather provides vital food and shelter for red grouse – which nibble the fresh young shoots but need mature plants in which to nest and take cover. The game shooting season is 12 August to 10 December but is unlikely to affect your walk. If approached by a human, grouse often freeze, invisible, until the last possible moment, relying on their camouflage. When they finally break cover, there's a dramatic flurry of wing-beats and a distinctive cackle of 'ge-back, ge-back, ge-back-back-back'.

Curlew

Much smaller birds, easily heard and spotted once you know what to look out for, are meadow pipits. They are the most common songbird, with a distinctive shrill call. Their upper parts are brownish with a pale underside, and you'll see their white outer tail feathers in flight.

Curlew may be sighted year-round in the Dales, but April to July is the breeding season for Europe's largest wading bird. Their streaky plumage helps to camouflage them on their moorland nests. In flight, its very long curved bill is visible. If you hear a shrill call with a rising whistle like an old-fashioned kettle, that is a curlew – the cry of the wild lonely places.

3·1 Barley to Sawley

Distance	**5·6 miles 9·0 km**
Terrain	**clear paths, stone steps, moorland and field paths with some stiles**
Grade	**stiff climb up Pendle Hill, gentler descent, then undulating paths**
Food and drink	**Barley, Downham, Sawley**
Summary	**a challenging ascent of the iconic Pendle Hill with its far-ranging panoramas, followed by pleasant farmland paths**

```
0·0                         3·7                          1·9      5·6
O————————————————————————————O————————————————————O————————O
Barley                      6·0              Downham    3·0    Sawley
```

- Our route begins in Barley, the small village from which George Fox seems to have made his journey up Pendle Hill in 1652. The Way officially starts at a fingerpost on Barley's main street, almost opposite the Methodist Church. How you reach it depends on how you arrive.

- If coming by car, use the car park (with toilets, Cabin café and map boards) just south of Barley village centre. Follow the Pendle Way on a roadside path north past the Pendle Inn (see below) to Barley Garage on the left side of the road. If arriving by bus, take the stop near the garage.

- About 50 m north of the garage, follow the Pendle Way fingerpost pointing up a footpath alongside the beck and over a few footbridges to join a minor road within 300 m of the start.

- Follow the road for 150 m to Ings End cottage where you bear right on a path for 550 m to Brown House Farm. Continue uphill following Pendle Way signs to Pendle House (with Cauldron snack bar), where a shortcut route up from Barley Lane lay-by joins our route from Barley village.

Pendle Inn, Barley

- The routes up Pendle Hill are becoming increasingly obvious ahead, and a 'Welcome to Pendle Hill' board confirms the choice you now make: gentler zigzag slope to the left or steep, direct stone steps to the right. We suggest you keep right to climb the well-maintained stone stairway.

- Take the strenuous climb at your own pace. The impressive view behind you over Barley and the reservoirs provide ample reason for frequent stops.

Stone steps on the ascent

- At the top of the climb you face a stone wall with a stile which marks our onward route. First, detour left to visit Big End (the summit) with trig point. Follow the line of the stone wall for under 100 m to reach a stone shelter with seating and a wall plaque about Fox (mile 1·4).

- Then, for the best view follow the well-made path for 400 m south to the trig point. Fox wrote of seeing the sea from this point, and on a clear day you see parts of Morecambe Bay to the west and north. To the north-north-west lies the Forest of Bowland, and moving clockwise you may glimpse the summits of Ingleborough and Pen-y-ghent distant to the north. The Pennines, Leeds and Bradford lie to the east, while to the south lies Manchester.

'As we travelled we came near a very great hill, called Pendle Hill, and I was moved of the Lord to go up... When I was come to the top, I saw the sea bordering upon Lancashire. From the top of this hill the Lord let me see in what places he had a great people to be gathered.'

George Fox climbed **Pendle Hill** in 1652, where he **had the vision** that inspired the **first followers of the worldwide QUAKER MOVEMENT**. Known as Quakers because they were said **'to tremble at the word of the Lord'**, the movement spread swiftly through Britain, Ireland and the American Colonies.

George Fox 1624-1691   {R*

WWW.RADICALSTRAIL.ORG.UK
DISCOVER THE RADICAL THINKERS OF PENDLE HILL

Wall plaque beside the shelter

South-east over the reservoirs

- After enjoying the summit, return by the path to the stone wall. If you are concerned about coping with a short stretch of harder terrain to visit Fox's Well, you can take a shortcut: go straight through the gate and follow the broad descent path, see map below and page 34 bullet 2.

- Otherwise, turn right for 60 m to the stone stile and climb over. Follow an indistinct trod path bearing right and descending to reach Fox's Well within 200 m. The square metal cover is just above the point where a small stream crosses your path.

- Lift the cover to find a metal tankard chained to the underside and water below. If you wish to drink from it, as Fox did, please purify the water first.

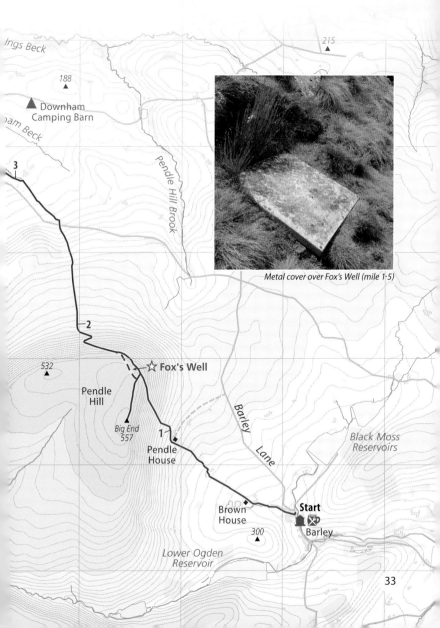

Metal cover over Fox's Well (mile 1·5)

- From Fox's Well continue on the faint path that contours Pendle Hill's grassy slopes. The steepish slope makes progress awkward at first, but after 100 m it joins a broad descent path.

- The broad path descends with a couple of zigzags before crossing the flatter, marshy moorland below. There are occasional Lancashire Way bootprint markers and Downham village is visible ahead to the left. The path drops to reach a road at mile 2·6.

- Cross the road and follow the fingerpost 'Public footpath Downham' over the stile. Then go down through woods to another stile, left over a small stream and up a few metres to a small barn.

- Locate the stile to the right and continue the route (waymarked Lancashire Way) down through woods and a series of gates and stiles to cross a small lane at Claydon House. A further kissing-gate takes you onto a good path through more woods.

- Cross a wooden bridge into a field and follow the right hand fence down past waymarkers and through two more kissing-gates. Follow Downham Beck down through a final meadow into the village at mile 3·7.

Pendle Hill from Downham Church

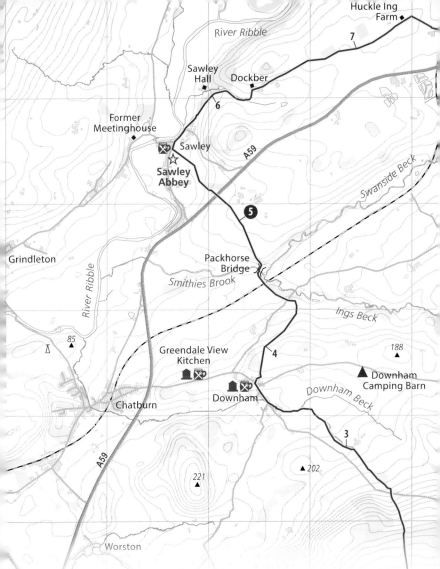

- Opposite the church is the Assheton Arms pub (formerly George & Dragon). This may be the alehouse where Fox overnighted after his vision on Pendle Hill. Should you wish to overnight in Downham (rather than Sawley) consider staying here or at Greendale View Kitchen B&B. The latter lies 600 m west on the Chatburn Road, and also offers meals.

- The Way turns right at the Assheton Arms on a signed footpath in front of the houses to a single gate into a field on your left, still waymarked Lancashire Way.

- Follow the path alongside the wall then, just after a group of five large trees, bear right as you descend. The path becomes clearer as the land falls away.

- Continue across the face of the hill to pass below two rocky outcrops and past a waymarker post until you reach a kissing-gate.

- Turn left onto the track and continue to the minor road ahead. Cross the road and go through a kissing-gate. Follow the path alongside the trees to a tunnel under the railway (mile 4·5).

Packhorse bridge over Smithies Brook

- Continue on the path alongside the woods and pass through an old gateway into a field. Bear right to cross a charming old packhorse bridge, then go over a stone step-stile. Take extra care in the wet as the bridge has no parapet.

- Continue straight ahead, then bear left uphill to a stile among some hawthorn trees on the skyline. Follow a clear path diagonally across the field to a stile in its far left corner.

- Follow the line of hawthorns to the next stile, then head a short distance to a metal farm gate with a wire fence.

- Continue on the path across the field to a stile at the main road (A59). Cross straight over this busy road with care and go through a kissing-gate into the field opposite.

- Follow Lancashire Way signs through further gates down an old tree-lined lane. The path fords a stream, crosses an old lane, goes through a kissing-gate and crosses the fields opposite.

- Pass through an old gateway onto the fields next to the ruins of Sawley Abbey, to reach its prominent stone archway. Turn right at the road to pass the Spread Eagle Inn. To detour to the former Sawley Meetinghouse (built in 1777, sold in 2017), turn sharp left on Sawley Road and cross the River Ribble, retracing your steps afterwards. To continue the Way, see page 37.

Ruins of Sawley Abbey

> ### Sawley Abbey
> This Cistercian abbey was founded in 1146 and the unusual proportions of its church reflect its fluctuating fortunes. After the dissolution in 1536-7 the monks moved out, the abbott was hanged and the valuables were stolen. Over the next three centuries, nearly all the good stones were removed and repurposed in local farms and cottages. The site is now cared for by English Heritage.

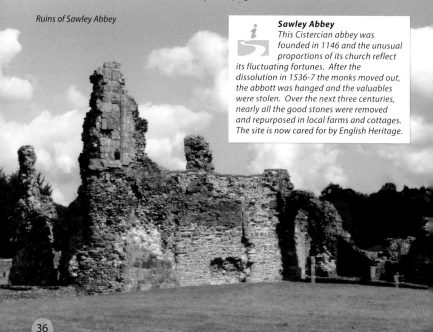

3·2 Sawley to Malham

Distance	16·8 miles 27·0 km
Terrain	fairly clear paths and tracks, but field sections can be boggy; woodland and riverside tracks; minor roads; lots of stiles
Grade	mostly easy going, but in places undulating with some short, steep descents and ascents
Food and drink	Sawley (pub), Gisburn (offroute), Paythorne (pub), Hellifield, Kirkby Malham
Summary	scenic walking across farmland and parkland, beside the River Ribble and through woodland; some longer sections of quiet minor roads

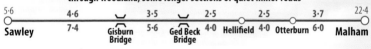

5·6 — Sawley — 4·6 / 7·4 — Gisburn Bridge — 3·5 / 5·6 — Ged Beck Bridge — 2·5 / 4·0 — Hellifield — 2·5 / 4·0 — Otterburn — 3·7 / 6·0 — 22·4 Malham

- From the Spread Eagle Inn, continue along Smiley Old Brow with the River Ribble on your left. After 150 m leave the road to go straight through the private gateway to Sawley Hall.

- After about 40 m, fork right up the tarmac lane following Ribble Way (RW) signs to a gate to a further tarmac lane.

- Turn left and continue steadily uphill passing behind Sawley Hall, partly hidden to your left. This section passes through the formal parkland of the Hall, and you may see deer.

Gate into the lane

- Cross a cattle grid and continue on the tarmac lane through the Dockber farms and onto the track to the left of the last barn. Follow the track uphill to a gate just short of a copse on the skyline.

- The path now goes into fields to your right, waymarked RW, and it passes through well-signed gates. Go through a stone gateway into a field containing a large metal sculpture dated 2019 and a modern stone circle.

- Cross the field – close to its high point – to a waymarked pair of gates, then follow the path ahead on the right of the field to a further gate. Continue along the tree-lined path to Huckle Ing Farm (mile 7·4).

Stone circle in the field

Gate in corner of the field

- Head straight on for 40 m to cross the tarmac farm lane and through a single metal gate marked RW. Follow the line of hawthorn trees and go through the gate in the corner of the field.

- The path now bears right, past a low brick structure and among three old trees, descending to a gate in the corner of the field at Gisburn Cotes Hall. To your right is a great view of Pendle Hill.

- Through the gate, leave the Hall to your right and head across the bridge over the railway. Turn left at the RW marker and head past some stone barns on your right.

- Follow the track to Gisburn Cotes Farm, go through the signed gate on your left towards a grass-covered bridge over the railway (mile 7·8).

- Over the bridge, bear right to join and follow the tree line to Long Holme Row.

- Cross the stile between two hawthorns to a ladder-stile over a wall. Pass through a single gate ahead, turn left onto the farm lane which crosses a small stream and go on to a stile and gate.

- Cross the stile and follow the fence line down to and through Steep Wood, arriving at the banks of the River Ribble.

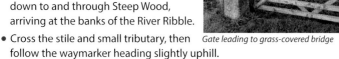

- Cross the stile and small tributary, then follow the waymarker heading slightly uphill.

Gate leading to grass-covered bridge

- Bear right at a fork, and head for the large oak tree on the skyline Waymarkers now direct you left along the top of the escarpment for about 300 m to a stile and gate.

- Follow the somewhat overgrown path ahead, keeping the fence on your right until you reach a bridge over a stream.

- Cross the stream and head slightly uphill to a stile at a fence junction. Over the stile, continue to follow the fence on your right for about 350 m to a single gate in the hedge.

- Pass through the gate and follow the clear path with the hedge now to your left, past an old barn (New Laithe) and the house, Wheatley (mile 9·2).

Oak tree on the skyline

- Pass through a kissing-gate and follow the tarmac lane round and uphill to Higher Laithe. Just before the farm, a fingerpost directs you to a gate and stile to the left of the buildings.

- From here the path is indistinct: walk to the fence corner with an old tree ahead and to your right, and head on across and down the field to a single gate.

- Through the gate, follow the path beside the stream to cross by a simple wooden plank footbridge. Go up through two kissing-gates and then bear right across and down the field to Coppice Farm.

Uphill to a stile at a fence junction

- Turn left to follow what is now also the Pennine Bridleway (PBW). Pass through the farm, taking the grassy path past a reindeer enclosure to join the driveway heading right. Follow it to Mill Lane.

Path past the reindeer enclosure

Driveway to Mill Lane

- At Mill Lane, turn left and continue downhill to Gisburn Bridge. Just before the bridge, turn right to follow PBW signs to the left of the houses. Follow the track uphill through the woods.

- As Gisburn Park main house comes into view, follow PBW signs to the right as the track skirts around the house to a PBW fingerpost 'Paythorne 1¾ miles'. Follow this track down through the woods to Stock Beck (mile 10·6).

- Cross the stone bridge and follow more PBW signs through the woods. Go up the track which may have a stream flowing down it.

Pennine Bridleway fingerpost

- Follow the track around the field edge to reach a gate close to the A682. Here, turn left and follow the PBW and RW along a fenced path beside the A682 main road, heading north.

- Upon reaching a gate, continue into the field, following the waymarkers. As the road alongside bends away to the right, pass through two further gates. Then head uphill to another gate on the right of the woods at the old earth workings of Castle Haugh (mile 11·5).

- The path ahead runs down the fence line and into the woods ahead.

- Continue into and through the woods, descending to meet the road at a bridge over the River Ribble. Cross the bridge and follow the road up to Paythorne.

Follow the fence into the woods

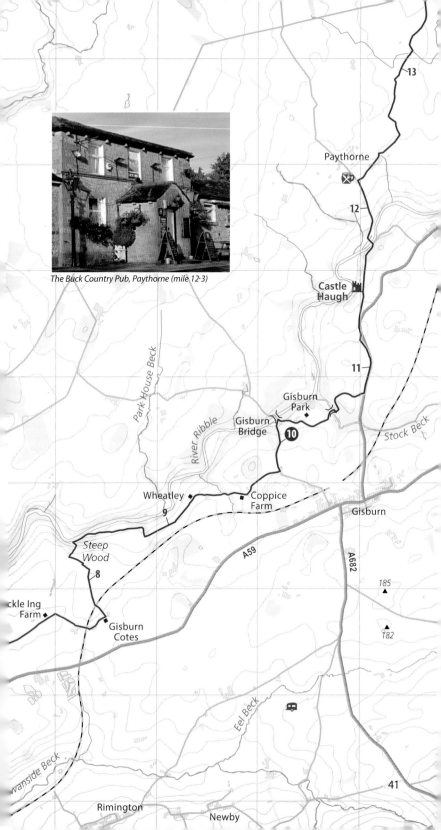

The Buck Country Pub, Paythorne (mile 12·3)

Paythorne

13

12

Castle Haugh

11

Park House Beck

River Ribble

Gisburn Park

Gisburn Bridge

10

Stock Beck

Wheatley

Coppice Farm

9

Gisburn

Steep Wood

8

A59

A682

185 ▲

ckle Ing Farm

Gisburn Cotes

182 ▲

Eel Beck

wanside Beck

Rimington

Newby

- Opposite the Buck Country Pub, turn right at the phone box to follow the bridleway past the buildings.

- Continue over a stone bridge and follow the track up and around the fields to a cattle grid. Turn left through a single gate, still following the PBW, and after 200 m turn right onto Ing Lane (a narrow path).

- Follow Ing Lane for about 500 m to a gated bridge at Paythorne Moor, perhaps with views of Pendle Hill behind you.

- Continue to follow PBW/RW signs to the left on a clear and well-marked path until you reach the road.

Follow the line of trees to rejoin the road

- Head along the road for about 150 m to Ged Beck Bridge and turn right at the PBW fingerpost. Cross the fields to a gate to the right of the large tree.

- Through the gate, continue on the right side of the field to a waymarker then turn left to pass along a line of trees to rejoin the road at mile 14.

- Turn right to follow this road for 1·3 miles (2·1 km) through Halton West to cross the Ribble by Halton Bridge. (Ignore the PBW and RW which leave the road within 600 m.)

- Just 80 m after the bridge, leave the road to follow the fingerpost for a footpath diagonally left across the fields. Go past a lone tree to the junction with the A682.

- Cross the main road to a stone step-stile, then head diagonally left across the next field to a stile in the wire fence.

Follow the fingerpost diagonally left

- Bear right to pass through a tunnel under the railway with a gate at its far end (mile 15·7). Continue to the farm ahead, ignoring the earlier blocked tunnel.

- Turn left onto the tarmac lane, join the B6253 and head into the centre of Hellifield. At the junction with the A65, turn right and, opposite the church, turn left into Haw Grove. Follow it up to the railway level crossing at mile 16·4.

- Cross the railway with care to enter the Yorkshire Dales National Park: see page 25. Continue on Hall Lane for 1·4 miles (2·2 km). The path undulates north-east across fields, passing Hellifield Haw (see page 44) and Wenningber Hill on the right.

- Descend to a gate in a wall to Dacre Lane (another track) where you turn right through the woods. After 0·9 miles (1·4 km) you reach the minor road into Otterburn.

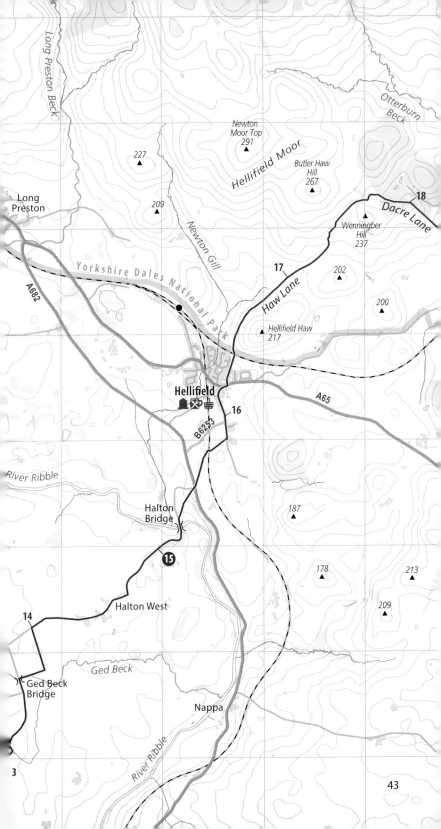

Long Preston Beck

Otterburn Beck

Newton
Moor Top
291

Hellifield Moor

Butler Haw
Hill
267

227 ▲

18

Dacre Lane

209 ▲

Long
Preston

Newton Gill

Wenningber
Hill
237

17

Haw Lane

202 ▲

200 ▲

Yorkshire Dales National Park

A682

●

Hellifield Haw
217 ▲

Hellifield

16

B6253

A65

River Ribble

187 ▲

Halton
Bridge

15

178 ▲

213 ▲

Halton West

14

209 ▲

Ged Beck

Ged Beck
Bridge

Nappa

3

River Ribble

Hellifield Haw

- Turn left and follow the road to then cross a bridge over the river. Turn left and then follow the old fingerpost for Kirkby Malham through some imposing black metal gates, past farm buildings and onto a track with a wall to your right.

- Continue to a wooden gate in the wall, pass through it and follow the fingerpost to the left across the field, heading uphill past a telegraph post near a tree to a large group of trees at the top.

- Follow the fence line above the woods to pass through a gate in the wall. Continue ahead to a wall corner and on to and through a gated step-stile.

- Follow the wall until it turns sharp right, then go straight on. The path is unclear: aim at a lone tree on the far hill to reach the road crossing at mile 20.

- Cross the road directly to a step-stile and follow the footpath uphill, gradually aiming for the left-hand corner of the woods on Warber Hill, and on to a gated step-stile.

- Head downhill keeping the wall to your right for about 350 m to a gated step-stile on your right, where the wall bends left.

- Cross the stile, and a bridge over a stream, then bear left up past a footpath marker to a stile across the track at the corner of the woods ahead.

- Head down the side of the woods for about 400 m to a kissing-gate into the woods. Pass through a second gate and down to a narrow footbridge across Kirkby Beck. After a short climb reach a lane where the Way turns right (mile 21).

Pendle Hill from Haw Lane (mile 17)

Malham Cove

☆

23

Malham

Sell Gill

22

Tranlands Beck

River Aire

Hanlith

Kirkby Malham

Kirkby Beck

21

Ingle Beck

Warber Hill
263

20

Park Hill
224

Interior of St Michael's, Kirkby Malham (mile 21)

180

18

Lane

19

192

Otterburn

Yorkshire Dales National Park

168

212

45

Bell Busk

Fell
6

- Take a tiny detour to visit St Michael's Church – the 'Cathedral of the Dales'. Its lych-gate leads off the lane through its graveyard to this lovely church that dates from the 15th century. Standing on a site where Christians have worshipped for over 1000 years, its doors are normally unlocked, it offers an informative free leaflet and a good guidebook is on sale.

- After the lych-gate, pass on your left (or visit) the Victoria Inn. Turn left at the corner to follow the main road through Kirkby Malham, past the phone box and around to the right.

- Stay on the road to the edge of the village, as far as a stone barn on the right (mile 21·3). Go up a few steps to a small gated stile, signed 'FP Malham 1 mile'. Much of this mile is grassy or muddy underfoot.

- Once over the stile, follow the wall briefly, then at a fingerpost 'Scalegill Mill' cross the field to another step-stile. This takes you onto a clear path with the River Aire running below, to the right.

Across the field to another step-stile

- Approach the Scalegill Mill cluster of buildings and pass to their left through a small gate. Keep ahead on a secluded path, at first beside what looks like a long thin pond, then crossing a stream by footbridge. Beyond Aire Head (where the River Aire rises) the stream to your right is Malham Beck.

- Your final approach to Malham is across a large field that you exit by a gate onto the main road. The National Park Centre is visible to the left: see page 25. The main village of Malham lies ahead and to the right.

- Malham is a popular tourist destination, and some of its houses have changed little since 1652. There are plenty of tea rooms, pubs and accommodation options.

Above: approaching Scalegill Mill
Below: path beside River Aire

3·3 Malham to Buckden

Distance	12·5 miles 20·1 km
Terrain	constructed path, limestone pavement and moorland tracks and paths; many stiles en route to Arncliffe
Grade	some steep climbs and a long stone stairway to the top of Malham Cove
Food and drink	Malham, Arncliffe (pub), Starbotton (pub), Buckden
Summary	scenic walking in the heart of the Yorkshire Dales following an 'M-shaped' route over into Littondale and then Upper Wharfedale

```
22·4        2·6        P    1·7              3·6             4·6       34·9
  ●──────────────────●──────────●──────────────────●──────────────────●
Malham    4·2   Watersinks 2·8 Middle House    5·8   Arncliffe   7·2   Buckden
                                Farm
```

- Walk north along Malham's main road past the Buck Inn, now following the Pennine Way (PW). Where the road forks, bear left and look for the signed Woodland Walk on the right, parallel to the road and beside Malham Beck.

- Soon emerge from woodland onto the road and follow it for a further 250 m to Town Head Barn where an NT sign directs you into Malham Cove on the right. The constructed path passes through fields, punctuated by gates and enlivened by resident cattle.

Fork left for Malham Cove

- The sheer cliffs of the cove are an impressive sight, and the beck a good place to spot dippers and wagtails. You may like to detour around the lower triangle of paths before settling into the main climb.

The cliffs of Malham Cove

South over Malham Beck from the top of the cove

- Our route stays with the Pennine Way (PW) up the stone steps on the left – over 400 of them – so pause to enjoy the views en route to the top. In addition to the wonderful limestone formations all around, from the top you may still see the distinctive shape of Pendle Hill to the south-west.

- The Way now turns right to cross the limestone pavement that stretches out across the top of the cove. The direct distance is only about 200 m, but take your time: the stones can be slippery and rare plants grow in the crevices: see page 29.

- After crossing the pavement, aim for a PW fingerpost which turns you left for 'Malham Tarn 1¼ ml'. Climb either of two stiles through a stone wall past the National Trust sign shown on page 49.

- Follow the clear, limestone-strewn path uphill to a stone step-stile and keep straight on up a rough, rocky staircase to a height of over 350 m (1150 ft) at the top of the 'Dry Valley' (Watlowes).

- At a PW fingerpost '1 mile to Malham Tarn' turn sharply back right and follow the path through a dramatic defile. The route then veers left and descends towards Watersinks car park. At the road, turn right for 100 m, then turn left through the car park to resume the PW northward at a fingerpost (mile 24·9).

Malham Tarn from the south-east

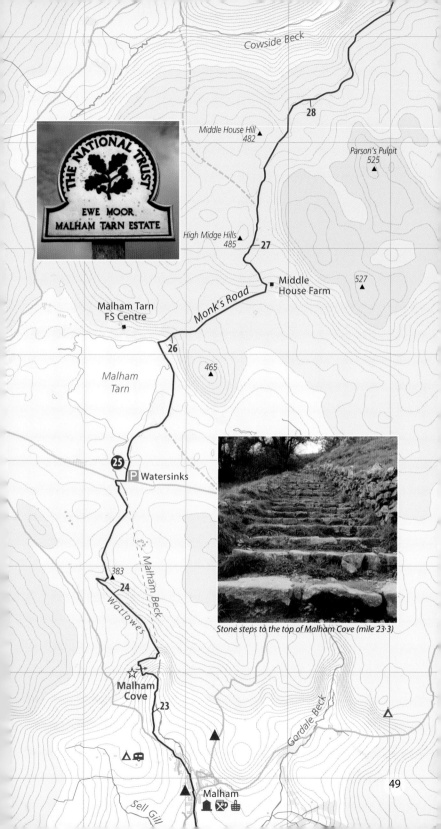

THE NATIONAL TRUST
EWE MOOR
MALHAM TARN ESTATE

Cowside Beck

28

Middle House Hill
482 ▲

Parson's Pulpit
525
▲

High Midge Hills ▲
485 — 27

Middle
House Farm ■

527
▲

Monk's Road

Malham Tarn
FS Centre ■

26

Malham
Tarn

465
▲

25
P Watersinks

383 ▲
24

Malham Beck

Wattowes

☆

Malham
Cove
23

Stone steps to the top of Malham Cove (mile 23·3)

▲

Gordale Beck

△

△🚐

49

▲ Malham
♜ 🍴 🏛
Sell Gill

- Continue towards the tarn shore on a grassy path, swinging briefly inland around a walled plantation before crossing to a PW fingerpost on the constructed track. Follow the track to and through a Malham Tarn Estate timber gate with red 'No vehicles' notice.

- Follow the track as it returns to the shore before approaching a gate with obscure fingerpost. The PW goes through it to Tarn House, but instead turn right before the gate, at mile 25·9.

- Head up the grassy hill following the fingerpost 'Middle House 2 ml'. You will follow Monk's Road, an old pack-horse path, all the way to Arncliffe, but signage is very sparse and does not use that name.

Fingerpost to Middlehouse

- At first, there are faint signs of a trod path which becomes a bit clearer as the ground rises, bending right to follow a fence. Crest the brow of the hill, and aim for Middle House Farm, now visible ahead.

- Approaching the farm, the path approaches a step-stile in the fence, but don't cross it (mile 26·6). Instead, follow the 'Arncliffe' blade of the fingerpost, pointing uphill, away from the farm.

- Pass through a gate in the stone wall and follow the rough, stony track as it bends left and right, then picks up the line of a stone wall as it descends towards trees and a cluster of stone barns: see photo below.

- After the barns, veer left towards a path junction at mile 27·3 that announces 'Arncliffe 2¾'. Bear right to follow the fingerpost northwards as the path becomes clearer – a pleasant grassy walk following a straighter course.

Fingerpost to Arncliffe (mile 27.3)

Cluster of trees near the stone barns

Gap in decrepit stone wall

- On the way to Arncliffe you cross eight or nine stiles in stone walls – a mixture of step-stiles – some gated, others not – and gap-stiles. In a couple of places the wall is so decrepit that there is no stile at all: see above.

- The long descent to Arncliffe includes some steep, rough downhill patches, and soon provides some great views over the village and Cowside Beck: see below. The final gate-stile deposits you in a grassy lane down which a stream may run in places.

- Lower down it becomes a tarmac lane that passes houses to emerge at the village green with the Falcon Inn (B&B and meals) on your right. The village is full of attractive stone buildings with a very fine church.

Stone pump, Arncliffe village green

- To continue the Way, head across the village green past the old stone pump to follow the narrow lane between houses and cross River Skirfare by a road bridge (mile 30·2).

- Within 120 m the road reaches a T-junction but you leave it, straight over a stile-gate into a field, following a discreet fingerpost marked Starbotton.

North-east over Arncliffe, with Cowside Beck

- Climb the first, very steep field and go over the step-stile into the second. Follow the trod path up to a fingerpost where you meet the bridleway and turn right uphill (mile 30·4).

- The bridleway is steep at first, but soon eases a little as it climbs above Brayshaw Scar, passing through a former gateway in the drystone wall. It's worth pausing from time to time to enjoy lovely views behind you over Arncliffe and Littondale.

Step-stile into second field

- Beyond the wall, there's a cottage ahead on Old Cote Moor. Ignore the track leading to it, and instead fork right at mile 30·9 on another track through the heather. Within 250 m at a track crossroads, go straight over heading for a false summit on the skyline.

- Afterwards reach a gate at the high point of 520 m. Follow the sign into the National Trust-owned Upper Wharfedale at mile 31·4.

- Continue straight ahead on the clear path between a fence and drystone wall, descending potentially boggy ground until the decrepit wall turns sharply left across the track. The track beyond is clear and broad: ignore any intersecting tracks.

- A steep descent finally leads to and through a hole in the wall ahead. Afterwards continue to descend, passing to the left of a large disused sheepfold. Go through a gate in the wall ahead. Panoramic views of Upper Wharfedale lie before you, with Starbotton and its fell ahead, and the River Wharfe meandering through its dale.

- After the gate, follow the track down to your left, passing through woods and meadows, until you reach a timber footbridge over the river. Take great care on this path as it can become slippery in the wet. If Starbotton is your goal, cross the River Wharfe by footbridge and follow the walled track to reach the road into the village.

- Otherwise continue on the well-marked Dales Way (DW) which stays to the west of the river. The path is easy going, and from here on you follow the DW almost all the way to Sedbergh.

- About 1·5 miles (2·5 km) after the Starbotton footbridge, the path follows the river banks closely. At mile 34·7 bear right, then turn right at the minor road (Dubb's Lane). For Buckden, cross the River Wharfe by road bridge.

Starbotton and Wharfedale from mile 32

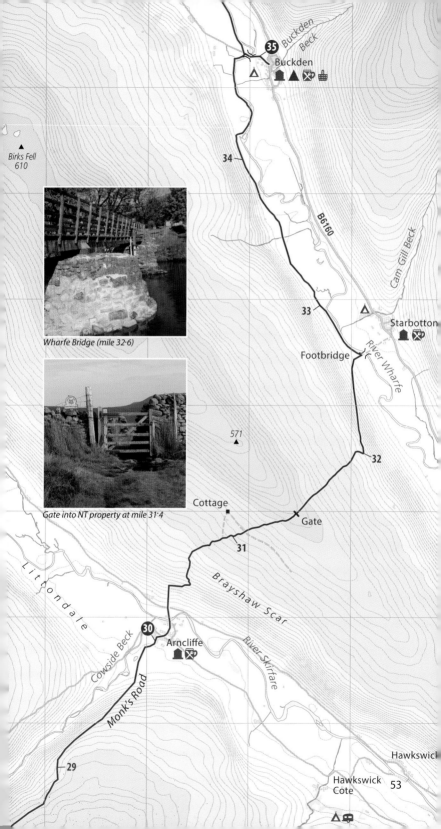

Buckden Beck

35 Buckden

Birks Fell
610

B6160

Cam Gill Beck

Wharfe Bridge (mile 32·6)

33

Starbotton

River Wharfe

Footbridge

571

32

Cottage

Gate

31

Gate into NT property at mile 31·4

Brayshaw Scar

River Skirfare

30

Arncliffe

Littondale

Cowside Beck

Monk's Road

Hawkswick

29

Hawkswick
Cote

53

3·4 Buckden to Far Gearstones

Distance	12·4 miles 20·0 km
Terrain	clear field paths, farm tracks and moorland path rising to an old Roman road; some stiles
Grade	steady climb leads to steeper section rising to 520 m (1700 ft), then steady descent to Far Gearstones
Food and drink	Hubberholme (pub), Ribblehead (1·5 miles off-route)
Summary	scenic walking along the Dales Way on a high-level route in Three Peaks country, with great railway views

```
34·9    2·7              2·3                2·7              4·7          47·3
Buckden  4·4  Yockenthwaite  3·7  Beckermonds  4·3  Swarthghyll  7·6  Far Gearstones
                                   Bridge
```

- At Buckden Bridge, cross the road and continue to follow the DW signed path along the riverbank for 0·6 miles (1 km). Turn right at the road and follow it to Hubberholme.

Buckden Stores

- Cross the river bridge and pass the church of St Michael and All Angels: see panel. Go left through a farmyard and continue left on the low-level DW path beside the churchyard, signed to Yockenthwaite.

- The Way stays close to the river for 1·6 miles (2·5 km) before rising to cross a wall on your right. Go ahead for 20 m, passing through two gates. Continue in front of the large farmhouse at Yockenthwaite (mile 37·8).

- Ignore the access road over the graceful bridge to your left and go through a gate amongst trees. Follow a farm track beside the river for 0·6 miles, passing a stone circle at mile 38·4.

> **Hubberholme Church**
> Set low beside the river, this fine Norman church has an ornamental oak rood loft dating from 1558 – a rare survivor of this type of feature: most such were destroyed. Oak pews by Robert Thompson bear his trademark carved mouse.

- Approaching a barn with an asymmetrical pitched roof, veer right on a rising path to a gap in the wall. Continue across the field, through a squeeze-stile and turn right.

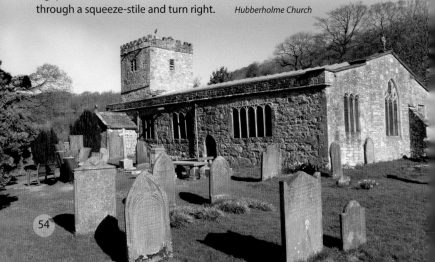

Hubberholme Church

Beckermonds

- Follow the wall around the field to a point opposite the stile. Cross a stream and a small enclosure to a farm access. Deepdale is on your right.
- Turn left at the public road. Cross Deepdale Bridge and turn right beside the river on a broad and uneven track.
- The track becomes a footpath that within 1·2 miles (2 km) reaches Beckermonds. Cross the footbridge and leave the riverbank by a walled lane.
- Turn right on the tarmac road, which climbs to the main road. Turn left onto the road at mile 40·2 towards Oughtershaw and the bleak grandeur of the fells.
- Continue for 1·4 miles (2·3 km) through Oughtershaw. At mile 41·3 the road bears right uphill: instead turn left onto a vehicle track signed Nethergill Farm and Swarthghyll Farm.
- At mile 42·7 bear right at Swarthghyll Farm, then go left in front of stock pens. Leave the farmyard through a metal gate onto rough pasture.

Oughtershaw Beck

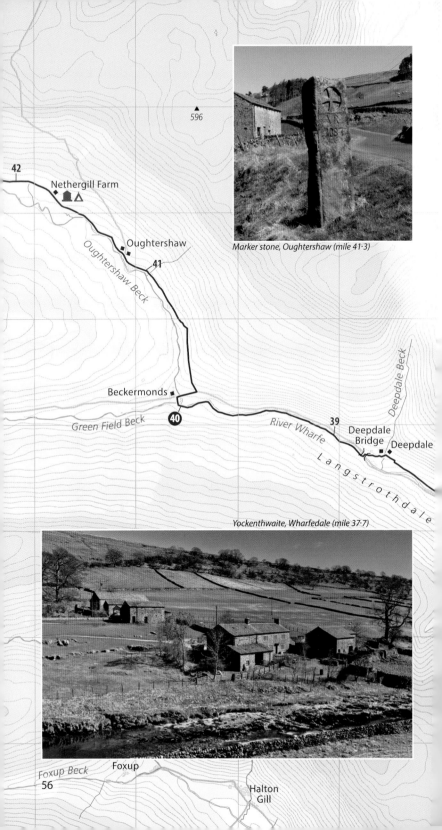

596

42

Nethergill Farm

Oughtershaw

41

Oughtershaw Beck

Marker stone, Oughtershaw (mile 41·3)

Beckermonds

40

Green Field Beck

River Wharfe

39

Deepdale Bridge

Deepdale

Deepdale Beck

Langstrothdale

Yockenthwaite, Wharfedale (mile 37·7)

Foxup Beck

Foxup

56

Halton Gill

- The Way is marshy and rutted at first, with a wall on your left. Pass through three plantations of young trees, each straddling a stream. Where the wall on your left ends, continue beside a fence.

- After the fence, pass through a narrow double wooden gate in the wall, then cross Far End Gill. Go up to Far End Barn, keeping it on your left and a wall on your right.

- At the next barn (Breadpiece Barn) follow the signs to turn right and go through the wall by timber gates.

Cam Houses

- Go left for a few metres, then climb right to a ladder-stile and somewhat decrepit wall.

- Cross Grainings Gill to another ladder-stile at the next decrepit wall. Cam Houses now comes into view.

- Cross a ladder-stile and pass in front of the first house. Turn right through a gap-stile in the wall, then turn left on the farm access road.

- Go left through a metal gate, then right in front of the barns. Leave Cam Houses through a gate, go over the stone step-stile to the right of a metal gate and into a short walled lane.

Ingleborough from Cam High Road

- Cross the field towards the right corner of the plantation. The path is indistinct in places and crosses several small streams. Ignore the gate in the wall on your right. Go through the plantation on the marked path.

- Cross a vehicle track and climb steeply at first to a stone cairn on the skyline at mile 45. Here you join Cam High Road, built by the Romans in AD 80 and now also used by the Pennine Way. In Fox's time Cam High Road was the main route across to the cattle market at Ribblehead. He may have followed another drove road from there to the head of Dentdale.

- At just over 520 m/1700 ft above sea level, the cairn marks the highest point of this section. The scenery is dominated by Yorkshire's Three Peaks: see the panel on page 59.

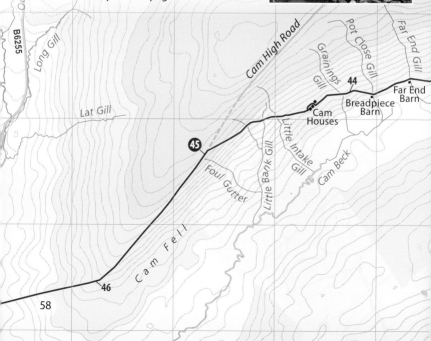

Ribblehead Viaduct

- Go left for 1·1 miles (1·8 km) to a marker post at a fork in the road. Here the Pennine Way turns left (south) but you keep ahead, still with the Dales Way. On a clear day you will spot the Ribblehead Viaduct distant to the west: see map page 61.

- Continue downhill and over a substantial wooden vehicle bridge spanning Gayle Beck to the main road (B6255). Go left towards Far Gearstones for 200 m, then at mile 47·3 turn right onto a tarmac track signed to Dent Head.

- The only nearby accommodation is Shepherd's Cottage, Winshaw at mile 47·6, a B&B that provides evening meals by arrangement. Otherwise there's the Station Inn and Gauber Bunk Barn at Ribblehead, reached after a further 1·5 miles (2·4 km) down the B6255: see page 61.

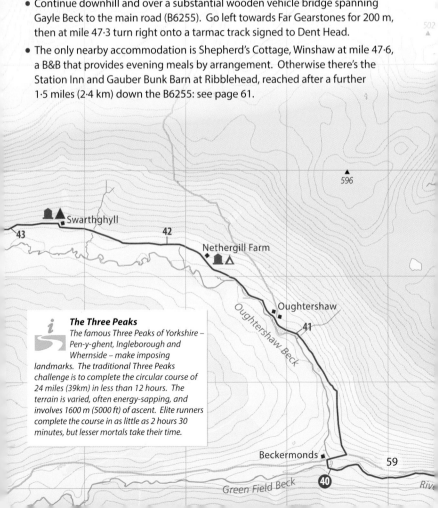

The Three Peaks

The famous Three Peaks of Yorkshire – Pen-y-ghent, Ingleborough and Whernside – make imposing landmarks. The traditional Three Peaks challenge is to complete the circular course of 24 miles (39km) in less than 12 hours. The terrain is varied, often energy-sapping, and involves 1600 m (5000 ft) of ascent. Elite runners complete the course in as little as 2 hours 30 minutes, but lesser mortals take their time.

3·5 Far Gearstones to Sedbergh

Distance	14·7 miles 23·7 km
Terrain	moorland and field paths, farm tracks, some stretches of minor road and riverside path, many stiles
Grade	a climb at first, then mainly level or moderate undulations
Food and drink	Dent, Sedbergh (wide choice)
Summary	follows the Dales Way past majestic viaducts and into Dentdale, with views of Whernside and later the Howgill Fells

47·3 — 3·1 — 2·1 — 4·1 — 3·2 — 2·2 — 62·0
Far Gearstones — 5·0 — Dent Head Viaduct — 3·4 — Lea Yeat Bridge — 6·6 — Church Bridge — 5·1 — Foot-bridge — 3·5 — Sedbergh

- If you stayed at Winshaw, the Way continues by climbing steps at the front to a narrow boggy path uphill. Turn right and follow a wall for 0·7 miles (1·1 km): skip the next bullet.

- If you stayed at Ribblehead, retrace your steps on the B6255 and take the tarmac track on your left signposted to Dent Head, opposite the track leading to Far Gearstones Farm. At Winshaw, pass the buildings on your right and climb steps to a narrow boggy path uphill. Turn right and follow a wall for 0·7 miles (1·1 km).

- Where the wall turns right downhill, go straight on. Within 200 m you reach the remains of a fingerpost marking the junction with Black Rake Road. Turn left to follow it for 1·2 miles (2 km). The track is mainly grassy or rocky, but boggy in places.

Packhorse bridge dwarfed by the viaduct

- Once you reach the road to Dentdale, turn left. Aye Gill Pike and Baugh Fell loom on the skyline, and far ahead you might glimpse the high fells of the Lake District. Follow the minor road, soon sighting ahead some of the ten arches of Dent Head Viaduct on the Settle-Carlisle railway.

- After about 1 km, the Way passes under this impressive Scheduled Ancient Monument. It was built 1869-75 from fossil-rich dark limestone known as Dent Marble. For a closer look, once across the river turn right off the road through a small gate: see photos above and below.

Train crossing Dent Head Viaduct, seen from the Way

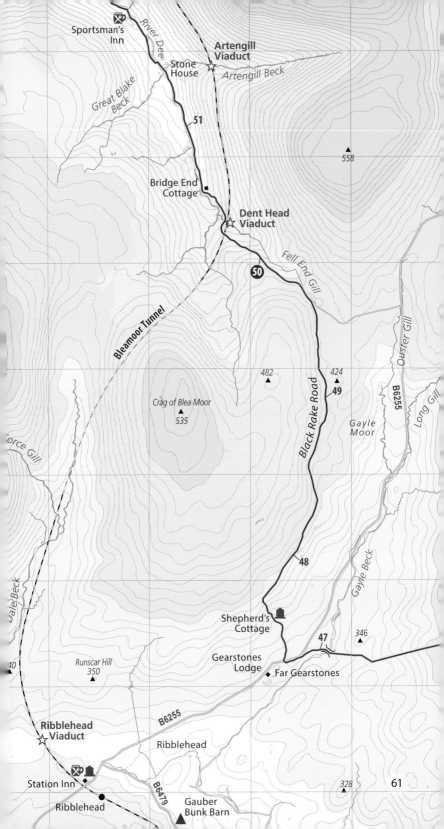

Sportsman's Inn

River Dee

Artengill Viaduct

Great Blake Beck

Stone House

Artengill Beck

51

558

Bridge End Cottage

Dent Head Viaduct

Fell End Gill

50

Bleamoor Tunnel

482

424

49

Ouster Gill

Crag of Blea Moor
535

Black Rake Road

Gayle Moor

B6255

Long Gill

Force Gill

Gayle Beck

48

Dale Beck

Shepherd's Cottage

10

Runscar Hill
350

47

346

Gearstones Lodge

Far Gearstones

Ribblehead Viaduct

B6255

Ribblehead

Station Inn

B6479

Ribblehead

Gauber Bunk Barn

328

61

West over Lea Yeat Bridge

- After 300 m, on the left past Bridge End Cottage, a timber gate leads to a pleasant picnic area by the riverside, with a sign welcoming Dales Way walkers.

- Over 1 mile (1·7 km) after Dent Head Viaduct, the road bends sharp left to cross the River Dee by a narrow bridge at mile 51·4. Look back for Artengill Viaduct, high on the Settle-Carlisle line to the east, also built from Dent Marble and also an Ancient Monument.

- From here the Sportsman's Inn is only 500 m along the road, and after a total of 2·8 miles (4·5 km) road-walking, you will arrive at Lea Yeat Bridge, Cowgill. Latterly from the road you have good views of the rocky river bed, sculpted into interesting forms by fast-moving water.

- The stone building at the right of the photo above served as Lea Yeat Meetinghouse from 1702 to 1911.

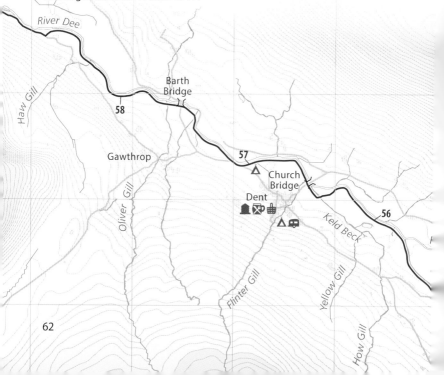

- Leave the road just before Lea Yeat Bridge through a gate to its left. The path hugs the riverbank for 500 m to Ewegales Bridge: do not cross.

- Continue on the narrow road, and after a further 500 m look for where you bear left up a track to Laithbank: the fingerpost is easily missed.

- Pass houses on your left and enter replanted woodland over a stile to follow a fairly distinct path.

- Before the next group of houses, turn right down natural steps and go through a gate. Cross the small field to a stile at its far-left corner.

Track bears left to Laithbank

- Taking the lower path, cross another stretch of replanted woodland and enter a field. Pass a stone barn on your left and continue through a small gate.

- With a wall on your right, descend past a barn to a concrete farm road. Turn left, and after 50 m turn right on a path. Cross the field to a gated stile near a tree. Continue to a stile in the far left corner of the next field.

- Go left along a lane for a few metres, then bear right to the large house of Coat Faw. Just in front of the house follow DW signs through a gate and across a small field. After the field, turn right to follow the wall and within 150 m rise to pass a house on your right.

- Cross a stile and a small stream. Pass a barn on your left, then immediately go left through a gateway. Continue in front of the farmhouse.

- Follow the access road, and at the sharp right bend go ahead through a gap in the wall. Pass a barn on your right, and ignore the vehicle track that descends to the right.

- Continue ahead through a gate and over a small stream. Keeping a barn on your left, leave the field and turn right downhill to the public road.

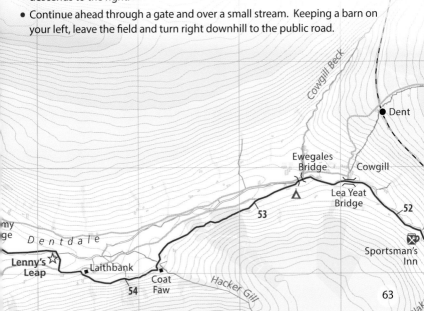

- Go left for 250 m. Turn right on a footpath and cross a stream to Lenny's Leap, a steep drop on your left.
- Cross the field to the river and go over the footbridge. Turn left to follow the riverbank for 650 m to Tommy Bridge (mile 55). Cross the river again and turn right.
- Go through a field gate and continue beside the river to the end of the next field. Ignore the vehicle gate and leave the field by a pedestrian gate further left.
- Climb the hill with the wall on your right. Where the wall bends right, continue straight ahead. Follow marker posts to a ladder-stile in the field corner which you climb to reach a road.
- Turn right along the road for a few metres, then turn right on a path signed to Church Bridge. Follow the small stream on your right and go through several gates until the stream meets the River Dee. The valley floor becomes wide and flat, and the Way follows the flood embankment.
- After 850 m ignore routes to each side at a ford. After a further 600 m veer left to cross Keld Beck at mile 56·5, then turn right to Church Bridge. To visit Dent village (see below), turn left along the road. Afterwards, either return to Church Bridge, or follow the minor road past the Heritage Centre for 600 m, then pick up a footpath across the fields to rejoin the Way at Barth Bridge (mile 57·6).

Dent village and Dentdale

Dentdale, although since 1974 assigned to the county of Cumbria, is a Yorkshire dale in miniature. Place names such as Coat Faw (from the Celtic *coed ffaw* – great trees) indicate ancient occupancy. Farms were established above the marshy valley floor and close to springs. Fields below the farms have been improved, whilst the land above remains as rough grazing.

Dent's former significance is recognised by the title 'Dent Town'. It clusters around its cobbled streets and 12th century parish church, St Andrew's. A medieval fair held in June drew people back home each year for a week of sports and celebration. Dent established its own grammar school early in the 17th century.

Dent Heritage Centre

Dent Marble, a fossil-rich black limestone, was quarried at Arten Gill. It was used for such diverse purposes as railway viaducts and a fireplace for the Tsar's Winter Palace in St Petersburg. In the late 19th century, cheap Italian imports forced it off the market.

Hand-knitting was at the heart of the economy in the 17th and 18th centuries, rising to a peak during the Napoleonic Wars. Everyone knitted as they went about their daily business or sat at home in the evenings. Schools were set up to teach knitting, not only to children but also to workers building the railway.

Try to call in at the Heritage Centre: phone 01539 625 800 for its opening hours or visit its website *www.dentvillageheritagecentre.com*.

- To continue the Way, cross the road at Church Bridge and follow the riverside path to Barth Bridge, with a brief stretch beside the public road.

- Beyond Barth Bridge the route remains close to the river, still on its south bank. After 1 mile (1·6 km) the field narrows and a sign points left towards a stile and a road.

- Head right along the road for 1·1 miles (1·7 km) to Brackensgill. Turn right to cross the river by footbridge – the last time you cross the River Dee – and continue up the narrow lane.

- After 250 m, cross the road into another lane (signed Millthrop) beside a high stone wall. The lane climbs steeply at first, and where it forks turn left, soon passing Gap Farm on your right.

- Go through a gate, across a field and through a wood, keeping to the wall on your left. The Way now follows a green bridleway for about 600 m, staying close to a wall on your right and climbing to 180 m. Sedbergh comes into view beneath the Howgill Fells.

- Go through a pedestrian gate and descend straight ahead. The path soon joins a vehicle track that descends to join the road at Millthrop.

- Bear right onto the road, then after 130 m turn left towards the main road. Turn right on it to cross the River Rawthey. On its far side, ignore the Dales Way which turns left, and instead go up the road into Sedbergh. Within 900 m you arrive at the lych-gate of St Andrew's Church: see below and page 71.

St Andrew's Church, Sedbergh

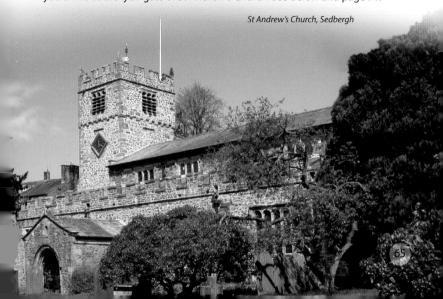

Sedbergh

Pronounced **sed**-ber, the town sits at the foot of the Howgill Fells. The name comes from the Old Norse for flat-topped hill. St Andrew's Church and Sedbergh's motte and bailey castle dominated the settlement in the 12th century. Its famous public (independent) school was established in 1525 and in recent times has become the town's largest employer.

Traditional industries were sheep farming and hand-knitting, and the town is a popular destination for walkers and other tourists. In 2006 Sedbergh reinvented itself as England's Book Town, joining Hay-on-Wye (Wales) and Wigtown (Scotland). For more about the town, visit *www.sedbergh.org.uk*.

Sedbergh is the end of our Way, but also the beginning of other journeys. In the next two sections we propose two day walks that are immersed in the town's Quaker heritage. Both start and end at St Andrew's Church: in this churchyard Fox preached from a high point near a yew tree, see page 18.

The circuit we propose in 3·7 includes his outdoor Pulpit from which he delivered his Sermon on the Fell. However Fox's 1652 journey ended not at Sedbergh but at Swarthmoor Hall, Ulverston, which became pivotal to the foundation of the Quaker movement. For this part of the journey, please refer to our sequel guidebook: see page 78.

Information centre, Sedbergh

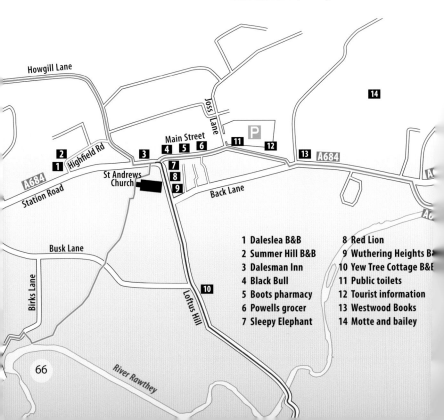

1 Daleslea B&B	8 Red Lion
2 Summer Hill B&B	9 Wuthering Heights B
3 Dalesman Inn	10 Yew Tree Cottage B&E
4 Black Bull	11 Public toilets
5 Boots pharmacy	12 Tourist information
6 Powells grocer	13 Westwood Books
7 Sleepy Elephant	14 Motte and bailey

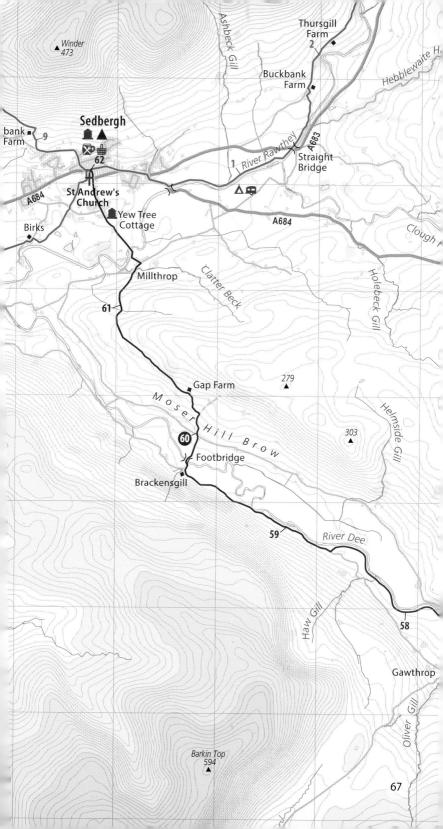

Winder
▲473

Ashbeck Gill

Thursgill Farm
2

Buckbank Farm

Hebblewaite H

bank Farm
9

Sedbergh
62

River Rawthey

A683

Straight Bridge

1

St Andrew's Church

A684

A684

Birks

Yew Tree Cottage

Clatter Beck

Clough

Millthrop

61

Holebeck Gill

Gap Farm

279
▲

Moser Hill Brow

303
▲

Helmside Gill

60

Footbridge

Brackensgill

59

River Dee

58

Haw Gill

Gawthrop

Oliver Gill

Barkin Top
594
▲

3·6 Sedbergh: to the Cross Keys

Distance	4·9 miles 7·9 km one-way, 9·8 miles 15·8 km round trip
Terrain	minor road, pavement, grassy paths, stony and farm tracks
Grade	mainly flat with some moderate undulations
Food and drink	Cross Keys Inn
Summary	linear route from Sedbergh, passing through farmland and fellside, with short sections of riverside and minor road

Unless you prefer to walk this route in both directions, you can take the bus one way: see page 78. It may be easier to catch your bus outward and return on foot without time constraint. Although the walking route follows a section of Wainwright's 'Pennine Journey', it is not signed as such.

- From St Andrew's Church, head 600 m east on Main Street and then follow the A683 to its junction with the A684, signed for Hawes and Garsdale.

- Follow the A684 for 300 m to the bridge over the River Rawthey. At a fingerpost, take the footpath to the left that follows the north bank of the river, signed '**Straight Bridge ¾ mile**'.

- At Straight Bridge, cross the road and continue on a footpath for 800 m to Buckbank Farm. Turn right onto the minor road for its final 300 m to

Fingerpost to Straight Bridge

Thursgill Farm (mile 2·3). Continue through Thursgill onto a good farm track leading to Fawcett.

- After 200 m, bear right at a fork in the track and descend steeply through the trees. After the steep descent, cross the bridge over Hobdale Beck and ascend steeply afterwards.

Cautley Spout: in the ravine at right

Bush Howe
623

Cautley Spout ☆

Cautley Holme Beck

Cross Keys
Temperance
Inn

The Calf
676

Bram Rigg Top
672

Great Dummacks
663

River Rawthey

4

Wardse

Ecker Secker Be

Bridge over Hobdale Beck (mile 2·5)

Hobdale Beck

3

Cautley

A683

Whinny Gill

Knott
429

Ashbeck Gill

Thursgill
Farm
2

Hebblewaite Hall Gill

Buckbank
Farm

edbergh

62

1   River Rawthey

A683

Straight
Bridge

drew's
urch

Yew Tree
Cottage

A684

Clough River

Millthrop

Clatter Beck

Holebeck Gill

61

- At Fawcett, follow the painted signs to pass around buildings on the left and go through the gate. Continue on the clear footpath following waymarkers on an undulating route through an avenue of hawthorn trees, fields and fellside covered with gorse and bracken.
- About 1·4 miles (2·3 km) after Fawcett, use the prominent gate to cross to the left side of the guiding wall. After a further 700 m, take the right hand of two five-bar gates and descend to cross Cautley Holme Beck via the timber footbridge.
- Turn right on the stone footpath ahead. If you were to follow it all the way to the left, you would reach the impressive Cautley Spout waterfall at the head of the valley; it's visible at the right of the photo on page 68.
- For the Cross Keys, bear right off the footpath after 500 m at a fork. Descend to re-cross the Rawthey on another footbridge. A short, sharp ascent takes you to the A683 where you turn right to reach the Cross Keys Inn within 50 m.
- If returning on foot, reverse the directions above and refer to map page 69.

The Cross Keys

There has been a building on this site since 1614, but the former farmhouse and coaching inn has been extended several times. Under its former name (High Haygarth) it belonged to Gervase Benson, Mayor of Kendal, colonel in Cromwell's army, Justice of the Peace and also a prominent Westmorland Seeker. Benson hosted George Fox during his stay in June 1652 and later became an active Quaker whose legal training was very valuable, especially on the subect of tithes and oath-taking.

Benson's first wife Dorothy was also a committed Quaker and one of the 'valiant sixty' men and women who spread the Friends' message in the mid 17th century. She was imprisoned in York for her beliefs and had to give birth to their son in prison in 1653. After she died in 1656, she was buried in the then garden at High Haygarth; after the house was extended, the dining area came to cover her grave, and she still lies beneath the floor.

The inn's temperance status dates from a tragedy that happened after a drunken evening in 1902. A group asked the landlord to see them home safely and after one of them fell into the River Rawthey, the landlord drowned while rescuing him. The drunkard survived, and his family bought the inn from the landlord's widow at the hugely inflated price of £900. They wrote into its title deeds that it could never sell alcohol.

Since 1949 the inn has belonged to the National Trust. The current tenants, Alan and Chris Clowes, have offered accommodation and meals here since 1997. Meeting this deeply Quaker couple and hearing their stories makes an unforgettable experience. Alcohol is allowed provided you bring your own. Check opening days, availability and how to book at *www.cautleyspout.co.uk*.

3·7 Sedbergh: the Quaker Trail

Distance	**9·4 miles 15·1 km**
Terrain	**minor roads with a couple of very short main road sections, paved/grassy paths, stony and farm tracks; many stiles**
Grade	**mainly level with some moderate to steep undulations**
Food and drink	**Sedbergh (wide choice)**
Summary	**clockwise circuit linking several key Quaker sites, starting from Sedbergh and visiting Brigflatts, Fox's Pulpit and Drawell Cottage**

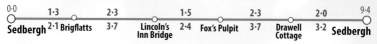

0·0 — **Sedbergh** 2·1 — 1·3 — **Brigflatts** 3·7 — 2·3 — **Lincoln's Inn Bridge** 2·4 — 1·5 — **Fox's Pulpit** 3·7 — 2·3 — **Drawell Cottage** 3·2 — 2·0 — **Sedbergh** 9·4

*This route is closely based (with permission) on the 2016 booklet **The Sedbergh Quaker Trail**: see page 78. We updated the directions and photos in 2021.*

- Facing the lych-gate of St Andrew's Church, walk 30 m to the right and take the paved path on your left down the outside of the church yard to Sedbergh School's sports fields.

- Turn right, and then left at a fingerpost 'Birks ½ mile'. Continue through the school grounds to a kissing-gate, and then down a grassy slope to a further gate onto Busk Lane.

- Cross the road directly and follow the gravel track signed 'Birks ⅓ mile'. As the track bears left at a broken wall junction, head straight on across the field until you reach a kissing-gate signed 'Birks'.

Lych-gate, St Andrew's Church

- Follow a clear path around the left side of Birks House until you reach a kissing-gate. Turn left onto the lane through Birks.

- Just after the double-bend in Birks pass through a kissing-gate in the hedge on your right with a fingerpost signed to Brigflatts. Ignore the sign to Toll Bar and instead cross the field, bearing left of the central rise, aiming for a stile between two gates.

- Cross the stile to follow a clear path at first alongside a wall, passing across the fields and through a series of taped-off horse paddocks. Aim for a small underpass on the dismantled Lune Valley railway line.

- Once through the underpass, cross the field ahead aiming for the large house (Rosebank) to the right of the whitewashed Brigflatts buildings.

West across the fields towards Brigflatts

Brigflatts Meetinghouse, date plaque inset

- Pass through a couple of gates to reach a lane with the Quaker burial ground opposite. Turn left down the lane to the Brigflatts Friends Meetinghouse: see the panel on page 73. Even if the Meetinghouse is closed when you visit, you may find tranquillity in its lovely gardens.

- Afterwards go back up the lane (180 m) to reach the main road (A683). Cross over with care and turn left to face oncoming traffic. After 300 m turn right onto a bridleway signed 'Ingmire Back Lane'.

> Public Bridleway
> Ingmire Back Lane

- The bridleway soon bears right at a field gate up a shady path between mature trees and an old stone wall. You almost reach the A684 road, but at mile 2·2 turn sharp left immediately onto a private lane signed 'Killington Bridge'.

- Cross the driveway access to the houses of Ingmire Court to a gate/stile and after another gate/stile follow the arrow on a fingerpost sending you half-right up the field past a waymarker post. Aim for the kissing-gate in the wall and go through it.

- Afterwards bear right to pass to the left of two clumps of trees and exit by the stile in the far right corner of the field, between two tall trees.

- Follow the yellow arrow to cross the next field diagonally, aiming for the right-hand end of the hedge.

- Climb the stile at the corner and turn sharp right to follow the fence northward, having now rejoined the Dales Way at mile 2·8.

Two tall trees at the far corner of the field

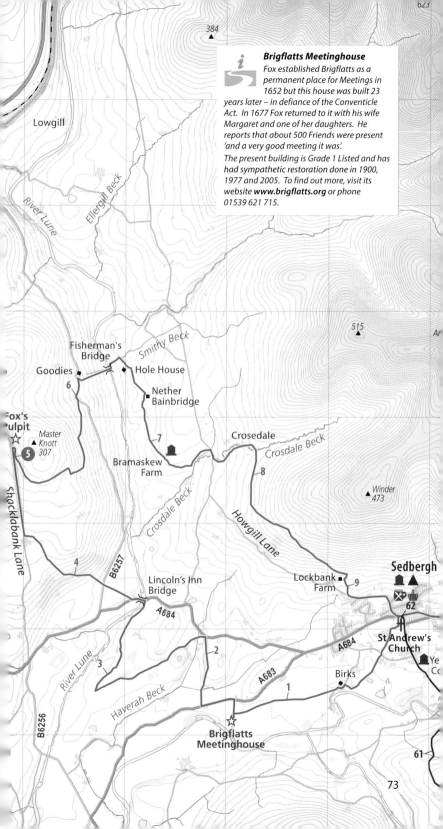

623

Lowgill

384 ▲

Brigflatts Meetinghouse

Fox established Brigflatts as a permanent place for Meetings in 1652 but this house was built 23 years later – in defiance of the Conventicle Act. In 1677 Fox returned to it with his wife Margaret and one of her daughters. He reports that about 500 Friends were present 'and a very good meeting it was'.

The present building is Grade 1 Listed and has had sympathetic restoration done in 1900, 1977 and 2005. To find out more, visit its website www.brigflatts.org or phone 01539 621 715.

River Lune

Ellergill Beck

515 ▲

Ar

Smithy Beck

Fisherman's Bridge

Goodies
6

Hole House

Nether Bainbridge

Fox's Pulpit
☆
5

Master Knott
▲ 307

7 ▪

Crosedale

Crosdale Beck

8

Winder
▲ 473

Bramaskew Farm

Crosdale Beck

Howgill Lane

Shacklabank Lane

B6257

4

Lincoln's Inn Bridge

A684

Lockbank Farm
9

Sedbergh
🏛 ▲
⊠ 🏚
62

3

River Lune

2

St Andrew's Church

A684

A683

Ye
Co

B6256

Haverah Beck

1

Birks ▪

Brigflatts Meetinghouse
☆

61

73

Howgill Fells from near Luneside Farm

- Go through a farm gate and follow the track to another gate beside the track, now with a high hedge.

- The next gate takes you into Luneside Farm. After passing among its buildings, follow a fingerpost for Lincoln's Inn Bridge. Climb a stile, then be sure to turn left to follow the field edges until you reach another stile with fingerpost on your left.

River Lune near Lincoln's Inn Bridge

- Climb that stile and follow the path going north with the River Lune below and to your left. If you are seeking a rest, there's an attractive stone beach near the arches of Lincoln's Inn Bridge.

- Climb the stile at the bridge, then cross the busy A684 road with care. Turn left along the narrow road bridge to cross the River Lune.

- Leave the road (and the Dales Way) barely 100 m after the bridge at a fingerpost pointing over a wall. Bear left up the field edge, cross a ladder-stile and continue up to a taller ladder-stile that deposits you on the B6257: take care, its treads are uneven and it may be overgrown.

- Cross the road to a farm gate with fingerpost and go straight up towards fenced woodland. At the woodland edge turn left along the fence for about 100 m to reach a stile (to the right of the more obvious gate).

- Once across the stile, bear left to climb diagonally through the woodland to its top boundary fence, which you cross by another stile.

- Bear left to climb the hill ahead, with a line of trees to your right. One of them bears a waymarker disc directing you to bear right uphill towards three trees. Aim to leave all three to your right and look for two farm gates.

Ladder-stile to the B6257

- Pass through the rightmost gate and aim diagonally across the field up to its far corner and pass through the gateway. Cross the next field diagonally, aiming for the stile at its far corner.

- Cross the stile and turn left along the farm track and go through a gate to reach the minor road (Shacklabank Lane) at mile 4·4. Turn right to follow it generally uphill with some views of a crag called Master Knott on your right.

Gate leading to Fox's Pulpit

- After 900 m of road, reach a roadside conifer that marks the gate into the rocky outcrop of Fox's Pulpit. (Adjacent is a gate into the churchyard of the former chapel of Firbank Fell.)

- Refer to page 18 for the background to Fox's Pulpit and its plaque celebrating his Sermon on the Fell (13 June 1652). Climb above the outcrop to stand on the inspiring viewpoint from which he spoke. This is a splendid place to linger.

- Afterwards, facing the pulpit from below, turn right along a fairly clear and dry path through the rushes for 100 m. At a fork, take the upper path and follow it onto a sheep trod contouring Firbank Fell, with Master Knott to the south.

- Shortly a wall and track come in from your right, which you will soon join. When the wall turns sharp right, follow it downhill until you reach a holly tree at the point where the wall becomes a fence.

- Follow a track heading downhill and left, away from the fence, for 60 m until you join a good track which merges from the right.

The Howgills seen from descent to River Lune

- Follow the track to the left as it gradually descends to fields. Pass through a gate and across two fields, then over a stile and down to reach the B6257 at mile 6.

- Turn left along the road for 200 m to a fingerpost at Goodies farmhouse, directing you to an old gate.

- Go through the gate and head straight downhill to a long footbridge over the River Lune, which you cross at mile 6·4.

- After the river, turn left for 50 m and then right beside a stream.

Footbridge over the River Lune

River Lune from the footbridge

- After going 100 m upstream, turn right onto the Dales Way at a fingerpost and pass through the cobbled and covered way through Hole House.

- After the farmyard and three farm gates, head straight up and over the steep hill ahead, following the fingerpost to Nether Bainbridge. Once over the hill, take the right-hand farm gate and cross the field to Nether Bainbridge Farm.

- A fingerpost in the left corner of the field directs you to a small gate in the wall to the right. Go through and take the track to the right, then pass through three gates into a field.

- Continue to a stile and through a group of walls linked by a small barn. Head directly up the hill ahead, looking across the valley to see Firbank Chapel. It was rebuilt in this location after a storm damaged its predecessor near Fox's Pulpit.

- Still on the Dales Way, take the ladder-stile over the wall ahead and go on to Bramaskew Farm which is a working beef and sheep farm and offers B&B.

- Go over a gated stile in a wall and follow the farm access road ahead to a gate. Leave the Dales Way to head straight on towards several farm buildings, including a concrete garage.

- Pass to the left of the garage, down a grassy passage and then to a gate. Drawell Cottage is to your right, just after the barn: see panel and photo.

> ### Drawell Cottage
> Now part of Bramaskew Farm, this historic cottage belonged to the Blaykling family who hosted Fox in 1652. It was from here that Fox departed to preach on Firbank Fell on 13 June 1652. Now offered for self-catering, the cottage contains various Quaker publications and artefacts.
>
> The barn was also the site of various events in Quaker history in 1665 and 1676. For cottage and farmhouse B&B phone 01539 621 529 or visit **www.drawellcottage.co.uk**.

Drawell Cottage

Descending to Sedbergh from the shoulder of Winder

- Just 20 m further on take the path through a wooden gate on the left. Head up to your left past a waymark, aiming for the rise ahead to a gate in the wall at the field corner. You are high above the small wooded valley made by Crosdale Beck.

- Keeping the fence to your right at first, head around the top of the valley. Go through a second gate, then over a stone step-stile. Exit onto Howgill Lane by a ladder-stile and turn right along the road. To continue the full circuit, leave Howgill Lane after 90 m at mile 7·5 and skip the next bullet.

- If you need a shortcut back to Sedbergh, instead stay on Howgill Lane, which forks left within 400 m to reach Sedbergh after a further 1·5 miles (2·4 km). Although the distance is only slightly shorter, this saves a climb and descent of about 80 m (260 feet) vertically.

- Otherwise, cross Crosdale Beck to reach a fingerpost and stile on the left. Go over the stile and follow the sign to Craggstone Wood up the steep hill ahead.

- Upon cresting the hill, follow the yellow-topped waymarker posts down to a fence above the beck.

- Then go up to two gates in the top left corner of the field. The ladder-stile and gate to the left lead up through woodland to two gates and onto the fell.

Entrance to the woodland

- Turn right and follow the wall line for 600 m up to its highest point. There is no distinct path, but stay roughly parallel to the wall until you eventually reach a gate in it with a track leading down to Howgill Lane.

- Continue past this gate and up to the next highest point of the wall where there is a further farm gate. From here, ignore the well-worn path uphill, and instead head off at an angle of 30° to the wall for about 50 m, aiming at a small tree on the skyline – almost due east.

- Then pick up a good track that bears right across open ground, crossing two streams and heading gradually downhill. Good views start to open out over Sedbergh and its surrounding fells and valleys as the track steepens and descends to Lockbank Farm at mile 9.

- Go through two gates into the farm, across the farmyard and onto a small access lane leading within 180 m to Howgill Lane.

- Turn left to follow the road for 600 m down to Sedbergh's Main Street, past the Dalesman Inn to St Andrew's Church.

4 Reference

Further reading

Boulton, David and Anthea (1998) *In Fox's Footsteps: a journey through three centuries* Dales Historical Monographs 0-9511578-2-5 out of print but obtainable from libraries or while stocks last from the Sleepy Elephant in Sedbergh.

The Boultons' detailed account of Fox's journey was the inspiration for our two guidebooks. They juxtapose Fox's route and life with the story of their 1994 walk in which they sought to replicate his journey. The result is full of thought-provoking insights and highly recommended. Why our route differs from theirs is explained here: *bit.ly/FW1-FF*

Fox, George (1694) *The Journal* available as a 720-page PDF download from
> *www.friendslibrary.com/george-fox/ journal*

This version was divided into chapters, edited and annotated by William Armistead in 1852. It benefits from a long preface by William Penn and a helpful glossary.

Hatton, Jean (2007) *George Fox: the founder of the Quakers* Monarch Books
> 978-1-85424-753-7

Hatton's biography is deeply researched with extensive footnotes and bibliography, but very readable because it's so well written and organised.

Smith, Dave (2016) *The Sedbergh Quaker Trail* This 16-page booklet describes the circuit which we follow in 3·7. It is still available as a separate publication from the Sleepy Elephant in Sedbergh at £1.50.

Friends Way 2
Margaret Fell's journey
(2023)

The route from Sedbergh to Swarthmoor Hall near Ulverston: for details, see *www.rucsacs.com/book/ friends-way-2*

Quakers in Britain

A comprehensive website is at
> *www.quaker.org.uk* with information about campaigns, events (including the Yearly Meeting), blogs and more, as well as letting you locate all Meetings in Britain by postcode. (For the island of Ireland, visit *quakers-in-ireland.ie* instead.)

Useful websites

We maintain a list of relevant links on our website: please visit
> *www.rucsacs.com/route-links/fw1*
to find many useful sites, including two inspiring videos and contacts for various places of interest along the Way.

Transport

For travel options from anywhere to anywhere, try *www.rome2rio.com*. The nearest airport to the route is Manchester:
> *www.manchesterairport.co.uk*

For journey planning and timetables within Britain, visit *www.traveline.info*

For buses to/from Sedbergh, visit
> *www.sedbergh.org.uk/travel/ getting-to-sedbergh-by-bus*

For services from Woof's (Sedbergh to Kendal via Oxenholme) see
> *woofsofsedbergh.co.uk/ ?Service_Bus_Times*

Rossendale operates the Ribble Country 66 and 67 bus services between Nelson and Clitheroe:
> *www.transdevbus.co.uk/rosso/services/ ROS/66*

DalesBus runs various relevant services for walkers, but routes and timetables differ seasonally: visit *www.dalesbus.org* and click through to their maps which also show the relevant rail services and stations, or visit
> *www.westerndalesbus.co.uk*

Weather and daylight forecasts

The Met Office is the authoritative source on weather in Britain. Visit its website
> *www.metoffice.gov.uk*

or download its app for mobile devices. When you need to know about cloud level, choose its **Specialist** forecasts tab, choose **Mountain** and click on the map.

For daylight and twilight hours anywhere in the world, up to 20 years ahead, visit *www.timeanddate.com/sun* and for this route enter Sedbergh.

Notes for novices

For those who lack experience in long-distance walking, we have prepared notes on choosing and using gear. Visit our website
> *www.rucsacs.com*
and scroll to the foot of page for *Notes for novices*.

Dates and calendars

In England during Fox's era, the Julian calendar was still in use: unlike our modern Gregorian calendar its year began on March 25 and ended on the following March 24, and it was also ten days behind. An added complication is that Quakers avoided the pagan Roman names for days and months, resulting in some confusion over dates.

For example, the 19th century gravestone shown on page 20 shows Fox's date of death '13th of 11th month 1690' which on the Gregorian calendar means he died on 23 January 1691. However, his date of birth was July 1624 Gregorian which should have been shown as 5th month (not 7th) Julian on his gravestone.

Acknowledgements

We warmly thank Rachel Muers, Professor of Theology, Leeds University, our expert Quaker consultant; Carole Nelson who suggested the project and secured sponsorship; Dave Smith and contributors to the *Sedbergh Quaker Trail* booklet; Annette Hirst and Annette Freeman, who rewalked a variant of the Boultons' walk in 2018; David Walker who helped with geology; Dr Joe Mellor who helped with route development; and Lindsay Merriman for painstaking proofreading.

We are most grateful to the following for helping to fund the route's development and this guidebook: Sedbergh and District Community Trust, Sedbergh Walking and Cycling Group, Christopher Robins Charitable Trust, the Yorkshire Dales NPA Sustainable Development Fund and Friends of the Lake District.

Photo credits

Mark Baker/*Wikimedia* p20; Martin Budgett pp6-7 & p44l, p8 (all 8), p37 (both), p38 (both), p39 (all 3), p40 (all 3), p42 (both), p52l, p53 (both), p54u, p63u, p68u, p69, p71 (both), p72l, p75 (lower 2), p76u, pp76-7, p77; Mike Clarke p68l, back cover; John H Darch/*geograph.org* p36u; Jan Fialkowski/*visitcumbria.com* p64; Tony Garofalo p14; Immanuel Giel/*Wikimedia* p31l; Chris Heaton/*geograph.org* p36l, p41; Tim Hill/*pixabay.com* p59u; Rude Health/ *geograph.org* p44u; William Hole (artist) p15; Library of Congress LC-DIG-pga-11433 p17; Jacquetta Megarry p9, p11 (all 8), p18l, p21, p24l, p29u, p31u, p32 (all 3), p33, p34u & mid, p45, p46 (all 3), p47u, p46 mid, p49 (both), p50 (all 3), p51 (all 3), p52u, p62, p70, p72 (lower 3), p74 (lower 2), p75u; Stephen Montgomery/*Wikimedia* p19; John Mottram/ *istockphoto.com* p29l; Mark Percy/ *geograph.org* p57; Pippa Rayner/YDMT p28l; Gordon Simm p26u, p28u, p30u; John Slater/*geograph.org* p55l; Dave Smith p72u, p76 mid; Peter Stott p54l, p55u, p56u, p58 (both), p74u; Robin Sutton p48l; Julian Thurgood *visitcumbria.com* p65; Visit Sedburgh p66.

We thank also *dreamstime.com* and its photographers for the following: Radomír Režný front cover, Davidmartyn title page & p48u, Peter Connolly pp4-5, p23, p60l, Georgesixth p8l, Georgios Kollidas p16, Jeanette Teare p18u, Jmci p22, Georgehopkins p24u, Kevin Eaves p25, Matauw p26l, BCritchley p26 mid, Davemhuntphotography p27u, Marcobarone p27 mid, Dalia Kvedaraite p27l, Gavin2162 p28mid, Digistockpix p29 mid, Thomas Langlands p30 inset, Anne Coatesy p30l, Drewrawcliffe p34l, George Robertson p47l, Kevin Eaves p56l, Paul Fleet p60u.

YORKSHIRE DALES
National Park Authority
Sustainable Development Fund

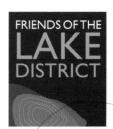

FRIENDS OF THE
LAKE
DISTRICT

Index